RANKING
THE
VICE PRESIDENTS

RANKING
THE
VICE PRESIDENTS

True Tales and Trivia,
from John Adams to Joe Biden

IAN RANDAL STROCK

Carrel Books

Carrel Books books may be purchased in bulk at special discounts for sales promotion, corporate gifts, fund-raising, or educational purposes. Special editions can also be created to specifications. For details, contact the Special Sales Department, Carrel Books, 307 West 36th Street, 11th Floor, New York, NY 10018 or carrelbooks@skyhorsepublishing.com.

Carrel Books® is a registered trademark of Skyhorse Publishing, Inc.®, a Delaware corporation.

Visit our website at www.carrelbooks.com.
10 9 8 7 6 5 4 3 2 1

Library of Congress Cataloging-in-Publication Data is available on file.

Cover design by Rain Saukas

Print ISBN: 978-1-63144-059-5
Ebook ISBN: 978-1-63144-061-8

Printed in the United States of America

For Dad.

CONTENTS

INTRODUCTION

When I was little, my mother hung a poster in the house, showing the Presidents' faces, names, and dates of office. I memorized it.

Soon after that, President Nixon announced his resignation, and my first political memory is asking my parents if that meant that Henry Kissinger would be President, because his was the only other name I knew. My parents explained to me about the Vice Presidency and that Gerald Ford was the new President.

Then I learned more about the Presidents and Vice Presidents—who they were, what they did, how they came to have those jobs—and I developed more and more of an interest in them. I began looking for commonalities, connections between the men who'd been President or Vice President, looking for patterns and signs. What characteristics did they share? What facets of their lives pointed toward their eventual elections? Could I calculate all the numbers to predict who would become the next President? Could I use the information I gathered to figure out whom they'd pick to be their running mates? Was there any chance I could earn those posts myself?

As it turns out, the answers are equivocal. Using those numbers, I was able to predict Barack Obama's election over John McCain and then his reelection over Mitt Romney. But I did not share those commonalities the Presidents seemed to have, so my odds of getting there are very long indeed.

While I was turning this lifelong interest in the Presidents into my first book (*The Presidential Book of Lists*, which Random House/Villard published before the election of 2008), I was also looking into the Vice Presidents, 14 of whom went on to serve as President. And I found the Vice Presidents to be no less interesting, individually or collectively.

Thus, I am pleased to present this book, originally conceived as a companion to my first, but definitely able to stand on its own. The Vice Presidents are a much more varied lot, and I hope you'll find them as fascinating as I do.

The Vice Presidents

The post of the Vice President of the United States is defined in Article II, Section 1 of the Constitution. Other than being available to succeed to the Presidency if necessary, the Vice President's sole Constitutional duty is spelled out in Article I, Section 3 ("The Vice President of the United States shall be President of the Senate, but shall have no Vote, unless they be equally divided.").

For the first four elections—before the rise of party politics—whoever came in second in the race for President was declared the Vice President. In the election of 1800, however, Presidential candidate Thomas Jefferson and Vice Presidential candidate Aaron Burr tied in the Electoral College, with 73 votes each, throwing the election to the House of Representatives and pointing out the need for what became the 12th Amendment, which provides for the election of the President and Vice President as a team.

The need for the White House, which was originally known as the Executive Mansion, was recognized when planning began for the capital city, during George Washington's term. But the Vice President was on his own for living arrangements (as is every other appointed and elected official in the government). The Vice President didn't receive an official residence until 1974, when Congress authorized the transformation of Number One Observatory Circle and its refurbishment. The house was built in 1893 for the superintendent of the US Naval Observatory and taken over by the Chief of Naval Operations in 1923.

Nelson Rockefeller, the Vice President at the time, already had a home in Washington and wasn't interested in moving into the new official residence, but he used it for entertaining. Walter Mondale was the first Vice President to live there.

Note on Usage

When it's appropriate to list the Vice Presidents by merely their last names, most of them are unique and present no problem. But there are several names shared by Vice Presidents or that Vice Presidents share with Presidents. In those cases, this book uses the following style: GClinton means George Clinton (who was Vice President from 1805 to 1812); BClinton is Bill Clinton (President, 1993–2001); RMJohnson is Richard M. Johnson (Vice President, 1837–41); AJohnson is Andrew Johnson (Vice President, 1865; President, 1865–1869); LBJohnson is Lyndon Baines Johnson (Vice President, 1961–63; President, 1963–69); HWilson is Henry Wilson (Vice President, 1873–75); and WWilson is Woodrow Wilson (President, 1913–21).

The term "First Lady" didn't come into widespread use until the late 1800s, and even into the early 1900s, its use was not universal. While it's generally used today to mean the President's wife, in point of fact, the government recognizes the term as referring to whoever serves as the "official White House hostess." In this book and *Ranking the First Ladies*, however, I've slightly modified the definition for simplicity's sake: in these pages, "First Lady" means any woman who was married to a President before, during, or after his term of office. I've also backdated the usage of the term to the beginning of the republic. Similarly, the term "Second Lady," in this book, refers to any Vice President's wife, whether they were married during his term of office or not.

In researching this book and its predecessor, I discovered that there are several methods of determining how closely two people are related. I've decided to use the method advocated by the National Genealogical Society, which seems the most common. In this system, to determine what degree of cousins two people are, count generations back to the common ancestor from each of the two people being compared. Using the person most closely related to the common ancestor, the degree of cousinhood (first, second, etc.) is one less than the number of generations between them. The degree of removedness (once removed, twice removed, etc.) is the number of generations difference between the two people being compared.

Common Ancestor	Child	Grandchild	Great-Grandchild	Great-Great-Grandchild	Great(3)-Grandchild
Child	Siblings	Nephew	Grand-Nephew	Great-Nephew	Great-Great-Nephew
Grandchild	Nephew	First Cousins	First Cousins, Once Removed	First Cousins, Twice Removed	First Cousins, Three Times Removed
Great-Grandchild	Grand-Nephew	First Cousins, Once Removed	Second Cousins	Second Cousins, Once Removed	Second Cousins, Twice Removed
Great-Great-Grandchild	Great-Nephew	First Cousins, Twice Removed	Second Cousins, Once Removed	Third Cousins	Third Cousins, Once Removed
Great(3)-Grandchild	Great-Great-Nephew	First Cousins, Three Times Removed	Second Cousins, Twice Removed	Third Cousins, Once Removed	Fourth Cousins

For example, James Madison and Zachary Taylor shared a pair of great-grandparents, Col. James Taylor and Martha Thompson. Their daughter Frances was President Madison's grandmother, while their son Zachary was President Taylor's grandfather. So we use the box on the left side for "great-grandchild" (James Madison) and the box at the top for "great-grandchild" (Zachary Taylor), and where those lines intersect, we see that they are second cousins. If, for another example, the common ancestors had been Zachary Taylor's great-great-grandparents, we would use that line on the top to find that the two Presidents were second cousins, once removed.

When discussing grandparents and grandchildren, I've used a parenthetical number for more than two greats, for simplicity's sake. Thus, great(5)-grandparents means great-great-great-great-great-grandparents.

Some older records are incomplete, notably birth dates for some women who married early Vice Presidents (for example). In cases where no date can be determined, those people have been ignored when calculating (for instance) averages of all the Vice Presidents' wives.

The information in this book is current as of December 31, 2015. For the latest news and updates, read my blog at uspresidents.livejournal.com or IanRandalStrock.com.

General Information about the Presidents

Name	Birth Date	Birthplace	Presidency	Death Date	Burial Place	Party	Vice President
George Washington	February 22, 1732	Westmoreland County, VA	April 30, 1789–March 4, 1797	December 14, 1799	Mt. Vernon, VA	Fed	John Adams
John Adams	October 30, 1735	Quincy, MA	March 4, 1797–March 4, 1801	July 4, 1826	Quincy, MA	Fed	Thomas Jefferson
Thomas Jefferson	April 13, 1743	Albemarle County, VA	March 4, 1801–March 4, 1809	July 4, 1826	Monticello estate, Charlottesville, VA	Dem-Rep	Aaron Burr / George Clinton
James Madison	March 16, 1751	King George County, VA	March 4, 1809–March 4, 1817	June 28, 1836	Montpelier estate, VA	Dem-Rep	George Clinton / Elbridge Gerry
James Monroe	April 28, 1758	Westmoreland County, VA	March 4, 1817–March 4, 1825	July 4, 1831	New York, NY (1831–58), Richmond, VA	Dem-Rep	Daniel D. Tompkins
John Quincy Adams	July 11, 1767	Quincy, MA	March 4, 1825–March 4, 1829	February 23, 1848	Quincy, MA	Dem-Rep	John C. Calhoun
Andrew Jackson	March 15, 1767	Waxhaws, SC	March 4, 1829–March 4, 1837	June 8, 1845	Hermitage estate, Nashville, TN	Dem	John C. Calhoun / Martin Van Buren
Martin Van Buren	December 5, 1782	Kinderhook, NY	March 4, 1837–March 4, 1841	July 24, 1862	Kinderhook, NY	Dem	Richard M. Johnson
William Henry Harrison	February 9, 1773	Charles City County, VA	March 4, 1841–April 4, 1841	April 4, 1841	North Bend, OH	Whig	John Tyler

Name	Birth Date	Birthplace	Presidency	Death Date	Burial Place	Party	Vice President
John Tyler	March 29, 1790	Charles City County, VA	April 6, 1841–March 4, 1845	January 18, 1862	Richmond, VA	Whig	
James Knox Polk	November 2, 1795	Mecklenburg County, NC	March 4, 1845–March 4, 1849	June 15, 1849	Polk Place, TN (1849–1893), Nashville, TN	Dem	George M. Dallas
Zachary Taylor	November 24, 1784	Orange County, VA	March 4, 1849–July 9, 1850	July 9, 1850	Louisville, KY	Whig	Millard Fillmore
Millard Fillmore	January 7, 1800	Locke Township, NY	July 10, 1850–March 4, 1853	March 8, 1874	Buffalo, NY	Whig	
Franklin Pierce	November 23, 1804	Hillsborough, NH	March 4, 1853–March 4, 1857	October 8, 1869	Concord, NH	Dem	William R. King
James Buchanan	April 23, 1791	near Cove Gap, PA	March 4, 1857–March 4, 1861	June 1, 1868	Lancaster, PA	Dem	John C. Breckinridge
Abraham Lincoln	February 12, 1809	near Hodgenville, KY	March 4, 1861–April 15, 1865	April 15, 1865	Springfield, IL	Rep	Hannibal Hamlin / Andrew Johnson
Andrew Johnson	December 29, 1808	Raleigh, NC	April 15, 1865–March 4, 1869	July 31, 1875	Greeneville, TN	National Union	
Ulysses Simpson Grant	April 27, 1822	Port Pleasant, OH	March 4, 1869–March 4, 1877	July 23, 1885	New York, NY	Rep	Schuyler Colfax / Henry Wilson
Rutherford Birchard Hayes	October 4, 1822	Delaware, OH	March 4, 1877–March 4, 1881	January 17, 1893	Oakwood Cemetery, Fremont, OH (1893–1915), Spiegel Grove, Fremont, OH	Rep	William A. Wheeler

Name	Birth Date	Birthplace	Presidency	Death Date	Burial Place	Party	Vice President
James Abram Garfield	November 19, 1831	Orange, OH	March 4, 1881–September 19, 1881	September 19, 1881	Cleveland, OH	Rep	Chester Alan Arthur
Chester Alan Arthur	October 5, 1830	Fairfield, VT	September 20, 1881–March 4, 1885	November 18, 1886	Menands (Albany), NY	Rep	
Grover Cleveland	March 18, 1837	Caldwell, NJ	March 4, 1885–March 4, 1889; March 4, 1893–March 4, 1897	June 24, 1908	Princeton, NJ	Dem	Thomas A. Hendricks / Adlai E. Stevenson
Benjamin Harrison	August 20, 1833	North Bend, OH	March 4, 1889–March 4, 1893	March 13, 1901	Indianapolis, IN	Rep	Levi P. Morton
William McKinley	January 29, 1843	Niles, OH	March 4, 1897–September 14, 1901	September 14, 1901	Westlawn Cemetery, Canton, OH (1901–1907), McKinley National Memorial, Canton, OH	Rep	Garret A. Hobart /Theodore Roosevelt
Theodore Roosevelt	October 27, 1858	New York, NY	September 14, 1901–March 4, 1909	January 6, 1919	Oyster Bay, NY	Rep	Charles W. Fairbanks
William Howard Taft	September 15, 1857	Cincinnati, OH	March 4, 1909–March 4, 1913	March 8, 1930	Arlington National Cemetery, VA	Rep	James S. Sherman

Name	Birth Date	Birthplace	Presidency	Death Date	Burial Place	Party	Vice President
Woodrow Wilson	December 28, 1856	Staunton, VA	March 4, 1913–March 4, 1921	February 3, 1924	Washington Cathedral, Washington, DC	Dem	Thomas R. Marshall
Warren Gamaliel Harding	November 2, 1865	Corsica, OH	March 4, 1921–August 2, 1923	August 2, 1923	Marion, OH	Rep	Calvin Coolidge
Calvin Coolidge	July 4, 1872	Plymouth, VT	August 3, 1923–March 4, 1929	January 5, 1933	Plymouth Notch, VT	Rep	Charles G. Dawes
Herbert Clark Hoover	August 10, 1874	West Branch, IA	March 4, 1929–March 4, 1933	October 20, 1964	West Branch, IA	Rep	Charles Curtis
Franklin Delano Roosevelt	January 30, 1882	Hyde Park, NY	March 4, 1933–April 12, 1945	April 12, 1945	Hyde Park, NY	Dem	John Nance Garner / Henry Agard Wallace / Harry S Truman
Harry S Truman	May 8, 1884	Lamar, MO	April 12, 1945–January 20, 1953	December 26, 1972	Truman Library, Independence, MO	Dem	Alben W. Barkley
Dwight David Eisenhower	October 14, 1890	Denison, TX	January 20, 1953–January 20, 1961	March 28, 1969	Abilene, KS	Rep	Richard Milhous Nixon
John Fitzgerald Kennedy	May 29, 1917	Brookline, MA	January 20, 1961–November 22, 1963	November 22, 1963	Arlington National Cemetery, VA	Dem	Lyndon Baines Johnson
Lyndon Baines Johnson	August 27, 1908	near Johnson City, TX	November 22, 1963–January 20, 1969	January 22, 1973	LBJ Ranch, Johnson City, TX	Dem	Hubert H. Humphrey

Name	Birth Date	Birthplace	Presidency	Death Date	Burial Place	Party	Vice President
Richard Milhous Nixon	January 9, 1913	Yorba Linda, CA	January 20, 1969–August 9, 1974	April 22, 1994	Nixon Library and Museum, Yorba Linda, CA	Rep	Spiro T. Agnew / Gerald Rudolph Ford
Gerald Rudolph Ford	July 14, 1913	Omaha, NE	August 9, 1974–January 20, 1977	December 26, 2006	Ford Library and Museum, Grand Rapids, MI	Rep	Nelson A. Rockefeller
James Earl "Jimmy" Carter	October 1, 1924	Plains, GA	January 20, 1977–January 20, 1981			Dem	Walter Mondale
Ronald Wilson Reagan	February 6, 1911	Tampico, IL	January 20, 1981–January 20, 1989	June 5, 2004	Reagan Library, Simi Valley, CA	Rep	George H.W. Bush
George H.W. Bush	June 12, 1924	Milton, MA	January 20, 1989–January 20, 1993			Rep	J. Danforth Quayle
William Jefferson Clinton	August 19, 1946	Hope, AR	January 20, 1993–January 20, 2001			Dem	Al Gore, Jr.
George W. Bush	July 6, 1946	New Haven, CT	January 20, 2001–January 20, 2009			Rep	Richard Bruce Cheney
Barack H. Obama	August 4, 1961	Honolulu, HI	January 20, 2009–			Dem	Joe Biden

General Information about the Vice Presidents

Name	Birth Date	Birthplace	Vice Presidency	Death Date	Burial Place	Party	President
John Adams	October 30, 1735	Quincy, MA	April 21, 1789–March 4, 1797	July 4, 1826	Quincy, MA	Fed	George Washington
Thomas Jefferson	April 13, 1743	Albemarle County, VA	March 4, 1797–March 4, 1801	July 4, 1826	Monticello, VA	Dem-Rep	John Adams
Aaron Burr	February 6, 1756	Newark, NJ	March 4, 1801–March 4, 1805	September 14, 1836	Princeton, NJ	Dem-Rep	Thomas Jefferson
George Clinton	July 26, 1739	Ulster County, NY	March 4, 1805–April 20, 1812	April 20, 1812	Kingston, NY	Dem-Rep	Thomas Jefferson / James Madison
vacancy			April 20, 1812–March 4, 1813				James Madison
Elbridge Gerry	July 17, 1744	Marblehead, MA	March 4, 1813–November 23, 1814	November 23, 1814	Washington, DC	Dem-Rep	James Madison
vacancy			November 23, 1814–March 4, 1817				James Madison
Daniel D. Tompkins	June 21, 1774	Scarsdale, NY	March 4, 1817–March 4, 1825	June 11, 1825	New York, NY	Dem-Rep	James Monroe
John C. Calhoun	March 18, 1782	Abbeville, SC	March 4, 1825–December 28, 1832	March 31, 1850	Charleston, SC	Dem-Rep	John Quincy Adams / Andrew Jackson

Name	Birth Date	Birthplace	Vice Presidency	Death Date	Burial Place	Party	President
vacancy			December 28, 1832–March 4, 1833				Andrew Jackson
Martin Van Buren	December 5, 1782	Kinderhook, NY	March 4, 1833–March 4, 1837	July 24, 1862	Kinderhook, NY	Dem	Andrew Jackson
Richard M. Johnson	October 17, 1780	Louisville, KY	March 4, 1837–March 4, 1841	November 19, 1850	Frankfort, KY	Dem	Martin Van Buren
John Tyler	March 29, 1790	Charles City County, VA	March 4, 1841–April 4, 1841	January 18, 1862	Richmond, VA	Whig	William Henry Harrison
vacancy			April 4, 1841–March 4, 1845				John Tyler
George M. Dallas	July 10, 1792	Philadelphia, PA	March 4, 1845–March 4, 1849	December 31, 1864	Philadelphia, PA	Dem	James Knox Polk
Millard Fillmore	January 7, 1800	Locke Township, NY	March 4, 1849–July 9, 1850	March 8, 1874	Buffalo, NY	Whig	Zachary Taylor
vacancy			July 9, 1850–March 4, 1853				Millard Fillmore
William R.D. King	April 7, 1786	Sampson County, NC	March 4, 1853–April 18, 1853	April 18, 1853	Selma, AL	Dem	Franklin Pierce
vacancy			April 18, 1853–March 4, 1857				Franklin Pierce
John C. Breckinridge	January 16, 1821	Lexington, KY	March 4, 1857–March 4, 1861	May 17, 1875	Lexington, KY	Dem	James Buchanan
Hannibal Hamlin	August 27, 1809	Paris, ME	March 4, 1861–March 4, 1865	July 4, 1891	Bangor, ME	Rep	Abraham Lincoln

Name	Birth Date	Birthplace	Vice Presidency	Death Date	Burial Place	Party	President
Andrew Johnson	December 29, 1808	Raleigh, NC	March 4, 1865–April 15, 1865	July 31, 1875	Greenville, TN	National Union (Dem)	Abraham Lincoln
vacancy			April 15, 1865–March 4, 1869				Andrew Johnson
Schuyler Colfax	March 23, 1823	New York, NY	March 4, 1869–March 4, 1873	January 13, 1885	South Bend, IN	Rep	Ulysses S. Grant
Henry Wilson	February 16, 1812	Farmington, NH	March 4, 1873–November 22, 1875	November 22, 1875	Natick, MA	Rep	Ulysses S. Grant
vacancy			November 22, 1875–March 4, 1877				Ulysses S. Grant
William A. Wheeler	June 30, 1819	Malone, NY	March 4, 1877–March 4, 1881	June 4, 1887	Malone, NY	Rep	Rutherford B. Hayes
Chester A. Arthur	October 5, 1830	Fairfield, VT	March 4, 1881–September 19, 1881	November 18, 1886	Menands (Albany), NY	Rep	James A. Garfield
vacancy			September 19, 1881–March 4, 1885				Chester A. Arthur
Thomas A. Hendricks	September 7, 1819	Muskingum County, OH	March 4, 1885–November 25, 1885	November 25, 1885	Indianapolis, IN	Dem	Grover Cleveland

Name	Birth Date	Birthplace	Vice Presidency	Death Date	Burial Place	Party	President
vacancy			November 25, 1885–March 4, 1889				Grover Cleveland
Levi P. Morton	May 16, 1824	Shoreham, VT	March 4, 1889–March 4, 1893	May 16, 1920	Rhinebeck, NY	Rep	Benjamin Harrison
Adlai E. Stevenson	October 23, 1835	Christian County, KY	March 4, 1893–March 4, 1897	June 14, 1914	Bloomington, IL	Dem	Grover Cleveland
Garret A. Hobart	June 3, 1844	Long Branch, NJ	March 4, 1897–November 21, 1899	November 21, 1899	Paterson, NJ	Rep	William McKinley
vacancy			November 21, 1899–March 4, 1901				William McKinley
Theodore Roosevelt	October 27, 1858	New York, NY	March 4, 1901–September 14, 1901	January 6, 1919	Oyster Bay, NY	Rep	William McKinley
vacancy			September 14, 1901–March 4, 1905				Theodore Roosevelt
Charles W. Fairbanks	May 11, 1852	Unionville Centre, OH	March 4, 1905–March 4, 1909	June 4, 1918	Indianapolis, IN	Rep	Theodore Roosevelt
James S. Sherman	October 24, 1855	Utica, NY	March 4, 1909–October 30, 1912	October 30, 1912	Utica, NY	Rep	William Howard Taft
vacancy			October 30, 1912–March 4, 1913				William Howard Taft

Name	Birth Date	Birthplace	Vice Presidency	Death Date	Burial Place	Party	President
Thomas R. Marshall	March 14, 1854	North Manchester, NH	March 4, 1913–March 4, 1921	June 1, 1925	Indianapolis, IN	Dem	Woodrow Wilson
Calvin Coolidge	July 4, 1872	Plymouth, VT	March 4, 1921–August 2, 1923	January 5, 1933	Plymouth Notch, VT	Rep	Warren G. Harding
vacancy			August 2, 1923–March 4, 1925				Calvin Coolidge
Charles G. Dawes	August 27, 1865	Marietta, OH	March 4, 1925–March 4, 1929	April 23, 1951	Chicago, IL	Rep	Calvin Coolidge
Charles Curtis	January 25, 1860	Topeka, KS	March 4, 1929–March 4, 1933	February 8, 1936	Topeka, KS	Rep	Herbert Hoover
John Nance Garner	November 22, 1868	Red River County, TX	March 4, 1933–January 20, 1941	November 7, 1967	Uvalde, TX	Dem	Franklin Delano Roosevelt
Henry A. Wallace	October 7, 1888	Adair County, IA	January 20, 1941–January 20, 1945	November 18, 1965	Des Moines, IA	Dem	Franklin Delano Roosevelt
Harry S Truman	May 8, 1884	Lamar, MO	January 20, 1945–April 12, 1945	December 26, 1972	Truman Library, Independence, MO	Dem	Franklin Delano Roosevelt
vacancy			April 12, 1945–January 20, 1949				Harry S Truman
Alben W. Barkley	November 24, 1877	Graves County, KY	January 20, 1949–January 20, 1953	April 30, 1956	Paducah, KY	Dem	Harry S Truman

Name	Birth Date	Birthplace	Vice Presidency	Death Date	Burial Place	Party	President
Richard Milhous Nixon	January 9, 1913	Yorba Linda, CA	January 20, 1953–January 20, 1961	April 22, 1994	Nixon Library and Museum, Yorba Linda, CA	Rep	Dwight David Eisenhower
Lyndon Baines Johnson	August 27, 1908	near Johnson City, TX	January 20, 1961–November 22, 1963	January 22, 1973	LBJ Ranch, Johnson City, TX	Dem	John Fitzgerald Kennedy
vacancy			November 22, 1963–January 20, 1965				Lyndon Baines Johnson
Hubert H. Humphrey	May 27, 1911	Wallace, SD	January 20, 1965–January 20, 1969	January 13, 1978	Minneapolis, MN	Dem	Lyndon Baines Johnson
Spiro T. Agnew	November 9, 1918	Baltimore, MD	January 20, 1969–October 10, 1973	September 17, 1996	Timonium, MD	Rep	Richard M. Nixon
vacancy			October 10, 1973–December 6, 1973				Richard M. Nixon
Gerald Rudolph Ford	July 14, 1913	Omaha, NE	December 6, 1973–August 9, 1974	December 26, 2006	Ford Library and Museum, Grand Rapids, MI	Rep	Richard M. Nixon
vacancy			August 9, 1974–December 19, 1974				Gerald R. Ford

Name	Birth Date	Birthplace	Vice Presidency	Death Date	Burial Place	Party	President
Nelson A. Rockefeller	July 8, 1908	Bar Harbor, ME	December 19, 1974–January 20, 1977	January 26, 1979	[cremated, ashes scattered at Tarrytown, NY]	Rep	Gerald R. Ford
Walter F. Mondale	January 5, 1928	Ceylon, MN	January 20, 1977–January 20, 1981			Dem	Jimmy Carter
George H.W. Bush	June 12, 1924	Milton, MA	January 20, 1981–January 20, 1989			Rep	Ronald Reagan
James Danforth Quayle	February 4, 1947	Indianapolis, IN	January 20, 1989–January 20, 1993			Rep	George H.W. Bush
Albert Gore, Jr.	March 31, 1948	Washington, DC	January 20, 1993–January 20, 2001			Dem	Bill Clinton
Richard B. Cheney	January 30, 1941	Lincoln, NE	January 20, 2001–January 20, 2009			Rep	George W. Bush
Joseph Robinette "Joe" Biden, Jr.	November 20, 1942	Scranton, PA	January 20, 2009–			Dem	Barack Obama

THE AVERAGE VICE
PRESIDENT

Averages tell us about groups and enable us to make predictions about any member of the group, but they can't tell us about the possibility for something new. Thus, any list of the average Vice President will not help us predict the odds of a woman becoming Vice President. After gathering all the data, preparing this book, and calculating all the comparisons, I was able to define the "Average Vice President." As with my Presidential book, it was one of my original goals to figure out what qualities these men shared and see if those characteristics might match myself (they don't).

In some cases, I had to omit certain Vice Presidents when calculating the averages (for instance, when calculating life span, the currently living Vice Presidents were not included). With these caveats, we can calculate the average Vice President. He (and looking at the 47 men who have held the office, the average Vice President is 100 percent male):

has a life expectancy of 72 years, 211 days (George M. Dallas is the most average in this respect, having lived 72 years, 174 days)

has a two-in-five chance of being named John, Charles, George, Richard, or Thomas

has a one-in-four chance of having been born in New York or Kentucky has a one-in-three chance of being buried in New York or Indiana (after he dies)

has a 27 percent chance of dying on the same day (but not necessarily the same year) as another Vice President

has a 6 percent chance of having no living predecessors

has a 17 percent chance of being born in the same year as another Vice President

has a 27 percent chance of dying in the same year as another Vice President

has 4.0 children (2.1 sons, 1.9 daughters)

is 7 years, 158 days older than his wife (Adlai Stevenson is the most average in this respect; he was 7 years, 77 days older than his wife)

has 1.2 wives

will die 2 years, 251 days after his wife (Levi Morton is the most average in this respect; he died 1 year, 275 days after his second wife [outliving his second wife, however, makes him unique]. Among Vice Presidents only married once, Richard Nixon is the most average; he died 304 days after his wife.)

has a 70 percent chance of being a lawyer

has a 53 percent chance of having been a member of the House of Representatives

has a 49 percent chance of having been a member of the Senate

has a 34 percent chance of having served in a state legislature has a 30 percent chance of having been a state Governor

has a 21 percent chance of having been some sort of businessman or entrepreneur

has a 15 percent chance of having attended Harvard or Yale

has a one-in-four chance of not being a college graduate

is 54 years, 293 days old when he takes office (Thomas Jefferson is the most average in this respect; he was 53 years, 325 days old when he took the oath of office)

has a 13 percent chance of serving two full terms

has a 39 percent chance of not serving until the end of the term (leaving a gap before the next Vice President takes office), either through death, resignation, or succession

will be Vice President for 4 years, 16 days.

THE VICE PRESIDENTS: LIFE AND DEATH

1. The Five Vice Presidents Who Lived the Longest

Three of the five longest-lived Vice Presidents went on to serve as President. Ford became President when Richard Nixon resigned eight months after appointing him Vice President. Adams, the sitting Vice President, was elected the second President upon George Washington's retirement. Truman succeeded to the Presidency when Franklin Roosevelt died in the third month of his fourth term. And the number six spot also belongs to a Vice President who became President: George H.W. Bush was the fourth sitting Vice President to be elected President, succeeding Ronald Reagan in 1989.

1. JOHN NANCE GARNER (1933–41). Born on November 22, 1868, he was Franklin Roosevelt's first Vice President and was dropped from the ticket when he opposed Roosevelt's campaign for a third term (Garner wanted to run for President himself). He was 98 years, 350 days old when he died on November 7, 1967. He lived more than five years longer than the longest-lived President.

2. LEVI P. MORTON (1889–93). Born on May 16, 1824, he died on his 96th birthday, in 1920.

3. GERALD R. FORD (1973–74). Born on July 14, 1913, he was the first person to be appointed Vice President (under the terms of the 25th Amendment, following Spiro Agnew's resignation), the first Vice President to become President upon his predecessor's resignation (Richard Nixon), and the longest-lived President. As Vice President, however, his 93 years, 164 days are only good for third place. He died on December 26, 2006.

4. GEORGE H.W. BUSH (1981–89). Born June 12, 1924, he was the first sitting Vice President to be elected President since Martin Van Buren did it in 1836, and is part of the only President and Vice President team to both reach the age of 90. He passed John Adams on February 14, 2015, and will pass Ford on November 23, 2017.

5. JOHN ADAMS (1789–97). Born on October 30, 1735, he was the first Vice President, the first sitting Vice President to be elected President, the first President to lose his bid for reelection, and, for 175 years, the longest-lived President (until Ronald Reagan eclipsed his record in 2001). He lost the title longest-lived Vice President in January 1915 to Levi Morton. Adams died on July 4, 1826 (during his son, John Quincy Adams's, term as President), aged 90 years, 247 days.

6. HARRY S TRUMAN (1945). Born on May 8, 1884, Truman is the second of Franklin Roosevelt's Vice Presidents on this list (after John Nance Garner). Truman served only three months as Roosevelt's third Vice President before Roosevelt died in office and Truman became President. When he died on December 26, 1972, he was 88 years, 232 days old. Truman is also #5 on the list of longest-lived Presidents.

WALTER F. MONDALE (1977–81), the senior living former Vice President, is three and a half years younger than George H.W. Bush. He'll pass Truman on August 24, 2016.

2. The Five Vice Presidents Who Died the Youngest

1. DANIEL D. TOMPKINS (1817–25). Born on June 21, 1774, he is also one of the five youngest Vice Presidents. He served two full terms under President James Madison and died three months after leaving office, on June 11, 1825, aged 50 years, 355 days. Tompkins had been in poor health for a decade and had suffered financial misfortunes dating from the War of 1812, which combined with his alcoholism to drive him to an early grave.

2. JOHN C. BRECKINRIDGE (1857–61). Born on January 16, 1821, he was the youngest Vice President ever when he and President James Buchanan took office. He only lived 54 years, 121 days, dying on May 17, 1875.

3. GARRET A. HOBART (1897–99). Born on June 3, 1844, Hobart was William McKinley's first Vice President. His death in office (after more than a year of suffering from heart failure), on November 21, 1899, cleared the way for McKinley to choose a new running mate in the election of 1900. That new Vice President, Theodore Roosevelt, became the youngest President ever when McKinley was assassinated in 1901. Hobart lived 55 years, 171 days.

4. JAMES S. SHERMAN (1909–12). Born on October 24, 1855, Sherman died in office on October 30, 1912. His death came one week before the election of 1912, in which he was a candidate for reelection. His death, however, probably didn't have a major effect on the election, because former President Theodore Roosevelt was running for reelection against Sherman's President William Howard Taft (Roosevelt's political heir). Democrat Woodrow Wilson took advantage of the split in the Republican Party to handily win the three-way race. Taft (and the deceased Sherman) came in third. Sherman lived 57 years, 6 days.

5. CHESTER A. ARTHUR (1881). Born on October 5, 1830, Arthur was Vice President for about six months. His President, James Garfield, was shot in July 1881, and died of the wound in September, vaulting Arthur into the Presidency. Arthur served his term, was not nominated for another, and then died on November 18, 1886, aged 57 years, 44 days. He is also #5 on the list of Presidents who died the youngest.

The youngest of the currently living Vice Presidents (all of whom are ineligible for this list) is AL GORE (1993–2001) who was born March 31, 1948.

3. The Five Vice Presidents Who Lived the Longest after Leaving Office

1. WALTER F. MONDALE (1977–81). Jimmy Carter's Vice President ran for the Presidency himself in 1984, but lost to Ronald Reagan's reelection landslide. Bill Clinton appointed him Ambassador to Japan in 1993. Mondale took the #1 spot on this list on April 22, 2014, when he was 86 years old.

2. RICHARD M. NIXON (1953–61). Nixon was the second-youngest Vice President ever, taking office before he turned 41. He served eight full years as Vice President, lost the Presidential election of 1960, and retired. He lived another 33 years, 92 days and won the Presidential elections of 1968 and 1972. Nixon died on April 22, 1994.

3. GERALD FORD (1973–74). Nixon appointed Ford Vice President when Spiro Agnew resigned in 1973. Ford served as Vice President for only 246 days before Nixon resigned and Ford succeeded to the Presidency. Ford is #3 on the list of longest-retired Presidents at just under 30 years. From the Vice Presidency, Ford was retired for 32 years, 139 days.

4. AARON BURR (1801–05). The third Vice President was the first to never be President. Aaron Burr was nearly President himself: he tied Thomas Jefferson in the Electoral College in the election of 1800, but Jefferson was chosen by Congress to be President. Their working relationship deteriorated throughout their four years in office, and by the election of 1804, the 12th Amendment had been adopted (providing for the President and Vice President to run as a ticket), and Jefferson chose George Clinton for the spot. Burr retired, was accused of treason at one point, and died on September 14, 1836, 31 years, 194 days after leaving office.

5. JOHN ADAMS (1789–97). The first Vice President, Adams was elected President in 1796, when George Washington announced his retirement. He served four years as President, lost his bid for reelection to Thomas Jefferson, and was retired from the Presidency for more than 25 years. He was the longest-lived President for a century and three quarters. He was retired from the Vice Presidency for 29 years, 122 days when he died on July 4, 1826.

6. HARRY S TRUMAN (1945). Franklin Roosevelt's third Vice President succeeded to the Presidency upon Roosevelt's death, about three months into his fourth term. Truman also won his own term as President and retired from that office on January 20, 1953. Truman is number five on the list of longest-lived Presidents. When he died on December 26, 1972, he had been retired from the Vice Presidency for 27 years, 258 days.

Factoring out those Vice Presidents who later became President, WALTER MONDALE maintains the #1 spot, and AARON BURR moves up to #2 on the list. Number 3 would be LEVI P. MORTON (1889–93), who was retired for 27 years, 73 days. Number 4 would be JOHN NANCE GARNER (1933–41), the longest-lived Vice President, who was retired for 26 years, 291 days. Number 5 would be HANNIBAL HAMLIN (1861–65), who was retired for 26 years, 122 days.

GEORGE H.W. BUSH (1981–89) was elected President in 1989. As Vice President, he's precisely eight years behind Mondale. He'll pass Truman for #6 on the list on December 26, 2016, when he's 92 years old, and John Adams on May 22, 2018.

JAMES DANFORTH QUAYLE (1989–93), Bush's Vice President, is four years behind Bush on this list and will pass Hamlin on May 22, 2019 (at the age of 72), Truman on December 26, 2020, and Adams on May 22, 2022.

ALBERT GORE, JR. (1993–2001) will pass Hamlin on May 22, 2027 (at the age of 79), Truman on December 26, 2028, and Adams on May 22, 2030.

RICHARD B. CHENEY (2001–09) will pass Hamlin on May 22, 2035 (at the age of 94), Truman on December 26, 2036, and Adams on May 22, 2038.

4. The Five Vice Presidents Who Died the Soonest after Leaving Office

More Vice Presidents died in office than Presidents. But of those who survived, more lived longer after leaving office. The Vice Presidents with the least time to enjoy their status as former Vice Presidents were:

1. DANIEL D. TOMPKINS (1817–25). The sixth Vice President was the youngest when he took office (he's currently the fifth youngest ever), and he's the shortest-lived of all the Vice Presidents, but he served eight full years in the office. He died on June 11, 1825, a scant 99 days after leaving office.

2. NELSON A. ROCKEFELLER (1974–77). Number five on the list of oldest Vice Presidents, Rockefeller was Vice President longer than he was a retired Vice President. He served for two years, 32 days and died on January 26, 1979, two years, 6 days after retiring from the office.

3. CHARLES CURTIS (1929–33). Curtis was Vice President to Herbert Hoover, who was the second longest-retired President (more than 31 years). Curtis, on the other hand, was only retired for two years, 341 days before his death on February 8, 1936. Curtis was also the oldest Vice President when he took office (69 years, 38 days) and is currently the second oldest ever.

4. ALBEN W. BARKLEY (1949–53). Barkley served during Harry Truman's second term and is the oldest Vice President ever (he was 71 years, 57 days old when he took office). He had been retired from the Vice Presidency three years, 101 days when he died on April 30, 1956.

5. THOMAS R. MARSHALL (1913–21). Woodrow Wilson's Vice President served eight years in that office and then was retired for only four years, 89 days. He died on June 1, 1925.

Tompkins's 99-day retirement was four days shorter than President James Polk's, but other than them, the least-retired Presidents died sooner than the Vice Presidents.

5. The Tallest and Shortest Vice Presidents

The tallest major-party candidate for President ever appears to be 6' 5" Winfield Scott, the Whig candidate who lost the election of 1852 to Franklin Pierce (the tallest President was 6' 4" Abraham Lincoln). The shortest were the victorious James Madison (who was elected in 1808 and 1812) and the defeated Stephen A. Douglas (who was the nominee of the Northern Democrats in 1860); they were each 5' 4" (John Adams, Martin Van Buren, and Benjamin Harrison are tied for #2 at 5' 6" each).

For Vice Presidents, the data is incomplete (we're missing numbers on 16 of the 47 Vice Presidents: George Clinton, Elbridge Gerry, Daniel Tompkins, John C. Calhoun, Richard M. Johnson, George Dallas, William King, Schuyler Colfax, Henry Wilson, William Wheeler, Garret Hobart, James S. Sherman, Thomas R. Marshall, Charles Curtis, John N. Garner, and Henry A. Wallace). But of those whose heights we do know:

The Five Tallest Vice Presidents

1. CHARLES W. FAIRBANKS, 6' 4" (Vice President under Theodore Roosevelt, who was 5' 10"). Fairbanks was a reporter, lawyer, financier, and then a Senator for eight years before being elected Vice President when Theodore Roosevelt ran for his own term as President. When Roosevelt retired at the end of the term, Fairbanks sought the nomination for President, but with Roosevelt's support, William Howard Taft was nominated and elected. Fairbanks went back to the practice of law, but in 1916, he won the nomination to again run for Vice President on the ticket with Charles Evans Hughes. They lost to Woodrow Wilson, and Fairbanks died two years later. Fairbanks, Alaska, is named for him.

2. LYNDON JOHNSON, 6' 3.5" (Vice President under John Kennedy, who was 6' 0"). After 12 years in the House of Representatives and 12 in the Senate, Lyndon Johnson sought the Democratic nomination for President in 1960, but lost out to Senator John Kennedy. Kennedy then chose Johnson as his running mate, and they won a very close election over sitting Vice President Richard Nixon and retired Senator and UN Ambassador Henry Cabot Lodge. In 1963, Kennedy was assassinated, and Johnson succeeded to the Presidency. He was elected to his own term in 1964 and was the second tallest President (after Abraham Lincoln).

3. HANNIBAL HAMLIN, 6' 3" (Vice President under Abraham Lincoln, who was 6' 4"). Former Representative and current Senator Hannibal Hamlin was nominated for Vice President at the Republican Convention of 1860, running with Abraham Lincoln, to make the tallest national ticket. In 1864, during the Civil War, Lincoln dropped Hamlin from the reelection ticket, fearing Hamlin wouldn't bring in enough votes in what was assumed to be a very close election. After leaving the Vice Presidency (and Andrew Johnson's succession to the Presidency following Lincoln's assassination), Johnson appointed Hamlin Collector of the Port of Boston, but Hamlin soon resigned in protest of Johnson's Reconstruction policy. Later, Hamlin was reelected to the Senate and then appointed US Minister to Spain by James Garfield.

4. THOMAS JEFFERSON, 6' 2.5" (Vice President under John Adams, who was 5' 6"). Thomas Jefferson lost the Presidential election of 1796, but under the original terms of the Constitution, whoever came in second in the election became the Vice President, so Jefferson served one term under John Adams, with whom he had split politically. In 1800, Jefferson defeated Adams, but by this time, candidates ran with Vice Presidential running mates. Jefferson wound up tying his running mate, Aaron Burr, and the election ended very contentiously with a decision by the House of Representatives. After they'd both retired from the government, Adams and Jefferson rekindled their earlier friendship. Jefferson and Burr, however, never reconciled, and Burr was charged with treason while Jefferson

was still serving his second term in office. (Jefferson is tied for #3 on the list of tallest Presidents.)

5 (tie). JOHN C. BRECKINRIDGE, 6' 2" (James Buchanan, 6' 0")

5 (tie). CHESTER ARTHUR, 6' 2" (James Garfield, 6' 0"; Arthur is tied for #5 on the list of tallest Presidents)

5 (tie). SPIRO AGNEW, 6' 2" (Richard Nixon, 5'11.5")

5 (tie). GEORGE H.W. BUSH, 6' 2" (Ronald Reagan, 6' 1"; Bush is tied for #5 on the list of tallest Presidents)

5 (tie). AL GORE, 6' 2" (Bill Clinton, 6' 2")

The Five Shortest Vice Presidents

1 (tie). JOHN ADAMS, 5' 6" (Vice President under George Washington, who was 6' 2"). Following the adoption of the Constitution, the first election was held. At the time, there were no candidates for Vice President: the person who received the second-greatest number of electoral votes for President would be the Vice President. George Washington's election was never in doubt (electors had two electoral votes each, and all 69 of them cast one vote for Washington). Eleven other candidates received votes, and John Adams won 34 of them (#3 was John Jay, with nine votes). Washington and Adams were reelected in 1792, and when Washington chose to step down after two terms, Adams won the close election of 1796 over Thomas Jefferson (Adams is tied for #2 on the list of shortest Presidents).

1 (tie). MARTIN VAN BUREN, 5' 6" (Vice President under Andrew Jackson, who was 6' 1"). After seven years in the Senate, two months as Governor of New York, two years as Secretary of State, and eight months as US Minister to the United Kingdom, Andrew Jackson chose Martin Van Buren as his Vice Presidential running mate for his second term (Vice President John Calhoun and Jackson had differences of opinion, and Calhoun was finishing his second term). Jackson and Van Buren were elected, and for a time, Jackson considered resigning to allow Van Buren to become President. But

he held on, and when Jackson retired, Van Buren was elected to his own term as President. (Van Buren is tied for #2 on the list of shortest Presidents.)

1 (tie). HUBERT HUMPHREY, 5' 6" (Vice President under Lyndon Johnson, who was 6' 3.5"). Following John Kennedy's assassination, Lyndon Johnson (the second-tallest Vice President) succeeded to become the second-tallest President. In 1964, Johnson ran for his own term as President, with Minnesota Senator Hubert Humphrey as his running mate. Humphrey and Johnson had both joined the Senate on January 3, 1949. Late in his term, Johnson announced his retirement, and Humphrey scrambled for the nomination to succeed him. He won the nomination, but lost the election of 1968 to Richard Nixon, who had been Johnson's predecessor as Vice President. In 1971, Humphrey returned to the Senate, and he died in that office in 1978.

4. AARON BURR, 5' 7" (Vice President under Thomas Jefferson, who was 6'2.5"). In the election of 1800, the candidates for President chose Vice Presidential running mates, though the Constitution had not yet been changed. Thus, while sitting Vice President Thomas Jefferson defeated his main opponent, President John Adams, 73-to-64 in the Electoral College, electors cast two votes, and none of Jefferson's electors thought to vote for someone other than his running mate, Aaron Burr, with their second votes. So Jefferson and Burr tied in the Electoral College, 73 apiece. Thus, the election was thrown to the House of Representatives, which took 36 ballots between February 11 and February 17, 1801, before they finally chose Jefferson over Burr. They took office on March 4, but Burr's refusal to step aside permanently ruined their relationship, and Jefferson chose George Clinton as his running mate for the election of 1804.

5. DICK CHENEY, 5' 8" (Vice President under George W. Bush, who is 5' 11.5"). Dick Cheney is the first White House Chief of Staff to later be elected to national office. He was Gerald Ford's Chief of Staff from November 1975 until Ford left office in January 1977. He went on to represent Wyoming

in the House of Representatives and then serve as Secretary of Defense under George H.W. Bush. Early in 2000, after George W. Bush had sewn up the Republican nomination for President, he asked Cheney (his father's Secretary of Defense) to run his Vice Presidential search committee. In July, after reviewing Cheney's findings, Bush chose Cheney himself to run for Vice President.

6. The Most Common Vice Presidential First Names

1. JOHN was shared by six Vice Presidents: Adams, Calhoun, Tyler, Breckinridge, and Garner. Calvin Coolidge's given first name was John. John is the second most common Presidential first name, shared by five Presidents (including three of these Vice Presidents who became Presidents).

2 (tie). CHARLES was shared by three Vice Presidents: Fairbanks, Dawes, and Curtis (and no Presidents).

2 (tie). GEORGE was shared by three Vice Presidents: Clinton, Dallas, and Bush (who later became the 41st President). George is the fourth most common Presidential name, shared by three Presidents.

2 (tie). RICHARD was shared by three Vice Presidents: Johnson, Nixon, and Cheney (who was commonly known as Dick).

2 (tie). THOMAS was shared by three Vice Presidents: Jefferson, Hendricks, and Marshall. Thomas is tied as the fifth most common Presidential name, shared by Jefferson and Wilson.

Henry, James, and William are the only other Vice Presidential first names shared by more than one Vice President. Henrys Wilson and Wallace, Jameses Sherman and Quayle (known as Dan), and Williams King and Wheeler. James is the most common Presidential first name, and William is the third most common Presidential first name.

The first Vice President to have a unique first name is third Vice President Aaron Burr. Twenty-four of the 47 Vice Presidents have unique first names (as do 19 of the 43 Presidents).

7. *The Most Popular States for Vice Presidents to Be Born*

Twenty-five different states (five more than the Presidents) were birthplaces to the 47 Vice Presidents (four more than the Presidents). Of the original 13 states, Connecticut, Delaware, Georgia, and Rhode Island have still not produced Vice Presidents. And 24 of the 47 Vice Presidents were born outside the original 13 states (the first was Kentucky's Richard M. Johnson, who was born in 1780 and served 1837–41).

1. NEW YORK was the birthplace for eight of the Vice Presidents, three of whom later became Presidents:

> George Clinton (1739)
> Daniel D. Tompkins (1774)
> Martin Van Buren (1782)
> Millard Fillmore (1800)
> William A. Wheeler (1819)
> Schuyler Colfax (1823)
> James S. Sherman (1855)
> Theodore Roosevelt (1858)

2. KENTUCKY birthed four Vice Presidents:

> Richard M. Johnson (1780)
> John C. Breckinridge (1821)
> Adlai E. Stevenson (1835)
> Alben W. Barkley (1877)

3 (tie). MASSACHUSETTS was the birthplace to three Vice Presidents, two of whom became President:

> John Adams (1735)
> Elbridge Gerry (1744)
> George H.W. Bush (1924)

3 (tie). VERMONT, the birthplace of two Presidents, was the birthplace of three Vice Presidents. Those two Presidents succeeded to the office from the Vice Presidency upon the death of their Presidents:

Levi P. Morton (1824)

Chester A. Arthur (1830)

Calvin Coolidge (1872)

Arthur may actually have been born in Canada, because his parents lived there for a time. If that's true, he would have been ineligible to be President, but since there was no debate at the time and since he's long dead, it's nearly a moot point. Vermont is generally accepted as his birthplace.

3 (tie). OHIO was the birthplace of three Vice Presidents (and seven Presidents):

Thomas A. Hendricks (1839)

Charles W. Fairbanks (1852)

Charles G. Dawes (1865)

8. The Most Popular States
for Vice Presidents to Be Buried

1. NEW YORK is the final resting place for nearly one-quarter of all Vice Presidents, which may not be surprising, because it's also the birthplace of the greatest number. Of the eight born in New York, one was buried in Indiana (Schuyler Colfax), and two non-New Yorkers (Chester Arthur and Levi Morton) were buried in the state. In New York, one can see the graves of:

George Clinton (died 1812)
Daniel D. Tompkins (1825)
Martin Van Buren (1862)
Millard Fillmore (1874)
Chester A. Arthur (1886)
William A. Wheeler (1887)
James S. Sherman (1912)
Theodore Roosevelt (1919)
Levi P. Morton (1920)

In addition to those nine, the body of Vice President Nelson A. Rockefeller, who died in 1979, was cremated, and his ashes were scattered on the Rockefeller Family Estate near Tarrytown, New York. Rockefeller is the only President or Vice President to not have a specific grave/final resting place, although there is a gravestone for him in the family cemetery.

2. INDIANA is the burial state of four Vice Presidents, none of whom were born in the state:

Schuyler P. Colfax (1885)
Thomas A. Hendricks (1885)
Charles W. Fairbanks (1918)
Thomas R. Marshall (1925)

Hendricks, Fairbanks, and Marshall are all buried in Crown Hill Cemetery, in Indianapolis (along with President Benjamin Harrison).

3. KENTUCKY is the burial state of three Vice Presidents, all of whom were born there:

Richard M. Johnson (1850)
John C. Breckinridge (1875)
Alben W. Barkley (1956)

Five states are the final resting places for two Vice Presidents each: ILLINOIS, MASSACHUSETTS, NEW JERSEY, TEXAS, and VIRGINIA.

8a. The Vice President Buried in Washington, DC

Fifth Vice President Elbridge Gerry, the second to die in office (on November 23, 1814), is the only one buried in Washington, DC. He is buried in the Congressional Cemetery.

9. The First and Last Vice Presidents to Be Born in the 1700s, 1800s, and 1900s

The first Vice President was also the first born. JOHN ADAMS (served 1789–97) was born October 30, 1735, nearly four years before fourth Vice President GEORGE CLINTON and even more years before every other Vice President.

Eleventh Vice President GEORGE M. DALLAS (served 1845–49) was the last Vice President to be born in the 1700s, when he was born on July 10, 1792, although WILLIAM R. KING (served 1853), the 13th Vice President, was the last person born in the 1700s to be elected (he was born April 7, 1786, before his three predecessors).

MILLARD FILLMORE, the 12th Vice President (served 1849–50), was the first to be born in the 1800s (although the last to be born in the 17th century); he was born on January 7, 1800.

The last child of the 1800s to serve as Vice President, ALBEN W. BARKLEY (served 1949–53), was born November 24, 1877, but his two predecessors were younger than he was. HENRY A. WALLACE (born October 7, 1888) was the last child to be born in the 1800s and later serve as Vice President (1941–45).

The first 1900s baby to be elected Vice President was RICHARD M. NIXON (served 1953–61), Barkley's successor, who was born January 9, 1913. Three of Nixon's successors were older than he was. NELSON A. ROCKEFELLER (born July 8, 1908) was the first child to be born in the 1900s and later become Vice President (1974–77).

10. The First and Last Vice Presidents to Die in the 1800s, 1900s, and 2000s

The only national officeholder to die in the 1700s was the first President, GEORGE WASHINGTON, who died in 1799. No Vice Presidents died in that century.

The first Vice President to die was GEORGE CLINTON, who was also the first to die in office. He passed away on April 20, 1812, having served from 1805. All three of his predecessors outlived him (John Adams and Thomas Jefferson died in 1826, and Aaron Burr in 1836).

The last Vice Presidential death in the nineteenth century was that of 24th Vice President GARRET A. HOBART (1897–99), who died in office on November 21, 1899.

The first Vice Presidential funeral in the twentieth century was for 27th Vice President JAMES S. SHERMAN (served 1909–12), who died in office on October 30, 1912. LEVI P. MORTON (served 1889–93) was the first person to serve as Vice President in the 1800s and live into the 1900s; he died on May 16, 1920, after his five immediate successors.

The last Vice Presidential funeral of the twentieth century was for 39th Vice President SPIRO T. AGNEW (served 1969–73), who died September 17, 1996. The last person to serve as Vice President in the 1900s and not survive into the twenty-first century was NELSON A. ROCKEFELLER (served 1974–77), who died on January 26, 1979.

The first Vice Presidential funeral in the twenty-first century was a Presidential funeral. Fortieth Vice President (1973–74), and 38th President (1974–77), GERALD R. FORD died on December 26, 2006. He is #3 on the list of longest-lived Vice Presidents, #2 on the list of longest-retired Vice Presidents, #3 on the list of longest-retired Presidents, and #1 on the list of longest-lived Presidents.

11. The Vice Presidents Who Shared Birthdays

Only one day saw the birth of more than one Vice President, but it was a triple. Hannibal Hamlin (1809), Charles G. Dawes (1865), and Lyndon Baines Johnson (1908) were all born on AUGUST 27.

And only one pair is so close as to miss sharing a birthday by one day. Adlai E. Stevenson was born October 23, 1835, and James S. Sherman was born October 24, 1855.

12. The Vice Presidents Who Shared Deathdays

JANUARY 13: Schuyler Colfax (1885) and Hubert Humphrey (1978)

JUNE 4: William Wheeler (1887) and Charles Fairbanks (1918)

JULY 4: First Vice President John Adams and second Vice President Thomas Jefferson died within hours of each other on July 4, 1826, the 50th anniversary of the signing of the Declaration of Independence. Fifteenth Vice President Hannibal Hamlin died on July 4, 1891.

NOVEMBER 18: Chester Arthur (1886) and Henry Wallace (1965)

DECEMBER 26: Harry S Truman (1972) and Gerald R. Ford (2006)

Additionally, several pairs missed sharing a death day by one day:

Calvin Coolidge (January 5, 1933) and Theodore Roosevelt (January 6, 1919)

Richard Nixon (April 22, 1994) and Charles Dawes (April 23, 1951)

And one particular week in November seems especially dangerous for Vice Presidents. Seven have died in the seven-day span from November 18 to 25:

Chester Arthur (November 18, 1886), Henry A. Wallace (November 18, 1965), Richard Johnson (November 19, 1850), Garret A. Hobart (November 21, 1899), Henry Wilson (November 22, 1875), Elbridge Gerry (November 23, 1814), and Thomas Hendricks (November 25, 1885).

13. The Vice Presidents Who Shared Last Names with Presidents

Three Vice Presidents had Presidential family names, but were never President and were not (as far as we can tell) related to the Presidents with whom they shared names. All of them served before the Presidents who shared their names.

George Clinton became Vice President when Thomas Jefferson won his second term as President, taking office March 4, 1805, and continued in the office as James Madison was elected. Clinton died in office on April 20, 1812. He shares his family name with Bill Clinton, who was President from 1993 to 2001.

Richard M. Johnson was Martin Van Buren's Vice President, serving from 1837 to 1841. He shares his family name with two unrelated Presidents, Andrew Johnson (1865–69) and Lyndon Baines Johnson (1963–69), both of whom were Vice Presidents who succeeded to the Presidency upon the death of their predecessors.

After a scandal during President Grant's first term, Vice President Schuyler Colfax was denied renomination. In his place, Senator Henry Wilson was nominated and won election as President Grant was handily reelected. Vice President Wilson took office on March 4, 1873, and soon suffered two strokes. He died in office on November 22, 1875. He shared his name with later President Woodrow Wilson (1913–21).

14. The Vice Presidents Who Outlived the Greatest Number of Their Successors

1. HANNIBAL HAMLIN (1861–65) outlived six of his successors before he died on July 4, 1891. Before his death, he saw the deaths of Andrew Johnson (his successor, Abraham Lincoln's second Vice President, who succeeded to the Presidency upon Lincoln's death) on July 31, 1875, Schuyler Colfax (January 13, 1885), Henry Wilson (November 22, 1875, in office), William Wheeler (June 4, 1887), Chester Arthur (November 18, 1886), and Thomas Hendricks (November 25, 1885, in office).

2. LEVI MORTON (1889–93) was the first of Hamlin's successors to outlive him. Morton outlived his five immediate successors, dying on May 16, 1920. His successors who predeceased him were: Adlai Stevenson (June 14, 1914), Garret Hobart (November 21, 1899, in office), Theodore Roosevelt (January 6, 1919), Charles Fairbanks (June 4, 1918), and James Sherman (October 30, 1912, in office).

3. JOHN ADAMS (1789–97). The first Vice President died on July 4, 1826. Adams's 29 post-Vice Presidential years puts him fourth on the list of longest-retireds, but only four of his successors predeceased him: George Clinton (April 20, 1812, in office), Elbridge Gerry (November 23, 1814, in office), and Daniel Tompkins (June 11, 1825). His successor, Thomas Jefferson (1797–1801), died a few hours before Adams (though Adams thought Jefferson survived him).

4 (tie). AARON BURR (1801–05). The third Vice President died on September 14, 1836, after Clinton, Gerry, and Tompkins (see above).

4 (tie). MARTIN VAN BUREN (1833–37). Van Buren died on July 24, 1862, and is #1 on the list of Presidents who outlived their successors; he outlived

five other Presidents. As Vice President, however, he only outlived three of his successors: Richard Johnson (November 19, 1850), John Tyler (January 18, 1862), and William King (April 18, 1853, in office).

4 (tie). RICHARD NIXON (1953–61). Nixon died on April 22, 1994, after being retired from the Vice Presidency for more than 33 years (he's #1 on that list), but he only managed to outlive three of his successors: Lyndon Johnson (January 22, 1973, he died while Nixon was President), Hubert Humphrey (January 13, 1978), and Nelson Rockefeller (January 26, 1979).

15. The Vice Presidents Who Were Older Than the Greatest Number of Their Predecessors

1. NELSON ROCKEFELLER. Born July 8, 1908, he came to office at the end of an era of younger Vice Presidents when he took office as Gerald Ford's Vice President in 1974. He was older than his five predecessors (three of whom also became President): Richard Nixon (born January 9, 1913, served 1953–61, he was the second-youngest Vice President); Lyndon Johnson (born August 27, 1908, served 1961–63); Hubert Humphrey (born May 27, 1911, served 1965–69); Spiro Agnew (born November 9, 1918, served 1969–73); and Gerald Ford (born July 14, 1913, served 1973–74). Rockefeller outlived Johnson and Humphrey.

2 (tie). WILLIAM KING. Born April 7, 1786, he was Franklin Pierce's Vice President, but died 45 days into his term in 1853. He was older than his three predecessors: John Tyler (born March 29, 1790, served one month in 1841, and then succeeded to the Presidency); George Dallas (born July 10, 1792, served 1845–49); and Millard Fillmore (born January 7, 1800, served 1849–50, and then succeeded to the Presidency).

2 (tie). THOMAS HENDRICKS. Born September 7, 1819, he was Grover Cleveland's first Vice President, but died 266 days after taking office, on November 25, 1885. He was older than three of his predecessors: John Breckinridge (born January 16, 1821, served 1857–61, he was the youngest Vice President); Schuyler Colfax (born March 23, 1823, he served 1869–73); and Chester Arthur (born October 5, 1830, he served six months in 1881 before succeeding to the Presidency). Hendricks outlived Breckinridge by 10 years and Colfax by 10 months.

4 (tie). Ten Vice Presidents were older than two of their predecessors when they came to office: GEORGE CLINTON, RICHARD JOHNSON, ANDREW JOHNSON, HENRY WILSON, WILLIAM WHEELER, THOMAS MARSHALL, CHARLES CURTIS, ALBEN BARKLEY, RICHARD CHENEY, and JOE BIDEN.

16. The Vice Presidents Who Had No Living Predecessors

1. JOHN ADAMS (1789–97), as the first Vice President, had no predecessors at all.

2. LEVI MORTON (1889–93) had no living predecessors from the time of Hannibal Hamlin's death on July 4, 1891 (Hamlin served 1861–65), until he left office on March 4, 1893.

3. THOMAS MARSHALL (1913–21) had no living predecessors from the time of Levi Morton's death on May 16, 1920, until he left office on March 4, 1921.

17. The Vice Presidents Who Had the Greatest Number of Living Predecessors

1. ALBERT GORE, JR., (1993–2001) had six living predecessors for one year, 92 days. Richard Nixon, Spiro Agnew, Gerald Ford, Walter Mondale, George H.W. Bush, and Dan Quayle were all alive at Gore's inauguration. Nixon died on April 22, 1994, and Agnew died two and a half years later, on September 17, 1996. The other four were alive for Dick Cheney's inauguration in 2001.

Seven other Vice Presidents had five living predecessors when they took office:

MILLARD FILLMORE (1849–50) had five living predecessors for one year, 27 days: John Calhoun (who died on March 31, 1850), Martin Van Buren, Richard Johnson, John Tyler, and George Dallas.

HANNIBAL HAMLIN (1861–65), for 320 days: Martin Van Buren, John Tyler (who died January 18, 1862), George Dallas, Millard Fillmore, and John Breckinridge.

HENRY WILSON (1873–75), for one year, four days: Millard Fillmore (who died on March 8, 1874), John Breckinridge, Hannibal Hamlin, Andrew Johnson, and Schuyler Colfax.

HUBERT HUMPHREY (1965–69), for 302 days: John Garner, Henry Wallace (who died November 18, 1965), Harry Truman, Richard Nixon, and Lyndon Johnson.

WALTER MONDALE (1977–81), for 358 days: Richard Nixon, Hubert Humphrey (who died January 13, 1978), Spiro Agnew, Gerald Ford, and Nelson Rockefeller.

Dan Quayle (1989–93), for his entire term of office: Richard Nixon, Spiro Agnew, Gerald Ford, Walter Mondale, and George H.W. Bush.

Joe Biden (2009–): When he took office, his five immediate predecessors (32 years' worth of Vice Presidents) were alive: Walter Mondale, George H.W. Bush, Al Gore, Dan Quayle, and Dick Cheney.

18. The Times There Were the Greatest Number of Living Former and Current Vice Presidents

There was only one time in US history when there were seven living former and current Vice Presidents, from January 20, 1993, until April 22, 1994. The seven were: Richard Nixon (1953–61), Spiro Agnew (1969–73), Gerald Ford (1973–74), Walter Mondale (1977–81), George H.W. Bush (1981–89), Dan Quayle (1989–93), and Al Gore (1993–2001).

Following Nixon's death was the seventh instance when there were six living former and current Vice Presidents, until Agnew's death on September 17, 1996.

The other seven times were:

1. March 4, 1849–March 31, 1850. From Millard Fillmore's inauguration until the death of John Calhoun (who served 1825–32). Also alive were Martin Van Buren (1833–37), Richard Johnson (1837–41), John Tyler (1841), and George Dallas (1845–49).

2. March 4, 1861–January 18, 1862. From Hannibal Hamlin's inauguration until the death of John Tyler (who served in 1841). Also alive were Martin Van Buren (1833–37), George Dallas (1845–49), Millard Fillmore (1849–50), and John Breckinridge (1857–61).

3. March 4, 1873–March 8, 1874. From Henry Wilson's inauguration until the death of Millard Fillmore (who served 1849–50). Also alive were John Breckinridge (1857–61), Hannibal Hamlin (1861–65), Andrew Johnson (1865), and Schuyler Colfax (1869–73).

4. January 20–November 18, 1965. From Hubert Humphrey's inauguration until the death of Henry Wallace (who served 1941–45). Also alive were John Garner (1933–41), Harry Truman (1945), Richard Nixon (1953–61), and Lyndon Johnson (1961–63).

5. January 20, 1977–January 13, 1978. From Walter Mondale's inauguration until the death of Hubert Humphrey (who served 1965–69). Also alive were Richard Nixon (1953–61), Spiro Agnew (1969–73), Gerald Ford (1973–74), and Nelson Rockefeller (1974–77).

6. January 20, 1989–January 20, 1993. From Dan Quayle's inauguration until his retirement from office. During his entire term of office, the other living former Vice Presidents were Richard Nixon (1953–61), Spiro Agnew (1969–73), Gerald Ford (1973–74), Walter Mondale (1977–81), and George H.W. Bush (1981–89).

7. January 20, 2009– . At Joe Biden's inauguration, his five immediate predecessors were all alive: Walter Mondale (1977–81), George H.W. Bush (1981–89), Dan Quayle (1989–93), Al Gore (1993–2001), and Dick Cheney (2001–09).

19. The Years During Which the Greatest Number of Vice Presidents Were Born

Four different years saw the births of two Vice Presidents each:

1782: John C. Calhoun (March 18) and his successor Martin Van Buren (December 5)

1819: William A. Wheeler (June 30) and Thomas A. Hendricks (September 7)

1908: Nelson A. Rockefeller (July 8) and Lyndon Baines Johnson (August 27)

1913: Richard M. Nixon (January 9) and Gerald R. Ford (July 14)

20. The Years During Which the Greatest Number of Vice Presidents Died

Three Vice Presidents died in 1875: John C. Breckinridge (May 17), Andrew Johnson (July 31), and Henry Wilson (November 22). Wilson died in office.

Four other years saw the deaths of two Vice Presidents:

1826: First and second and Vice Presidents John Adams and Thomas Jefferson died within hours of each other on the 50th anniversary of the signing of the Declaration of Independence, July 4, 1826.

1850: John C. Calhoun (March 31) and Richard M. Johnson (November 19)

1862: Martin Van Buren (July 24) and John Tyler (January 18)

1885: Schuyler Colfax (January 13) and Thomas A. Hendricks (November 25)

21. Presidential Terms During Which the Greatest Number of Vice Presidents Died

Two Presidents have seen the deaths of four Vice Presidents during their terms of office:

1 (tie). ULYSSES GRANT. During his eight-year term in the White House (1869–77), four Vice Presidents (two of whom had also been President) died. Millard Fillmore (who had been Vice President from 1849 to 1850) died on March 8, 1874; John C. Breckinridge (1857–61) died on May 17, 1875; Andrew Johnson (1865) died on July 31, 1875; and Grant's second Vice President, Henry Wilson, died in office on November 22, 1875.

1 (tie). WOODROW WILSON. During his eight-year term in the White House (1913–21), four Vice Presidents (one of whom had also been President) died. Adlai E. Stevenson (1893–97) died on June 14, 1914; Charles W. Fairbanks (Theodore Roosevelt's Vice President from 1905 to 1909) died on June 4, 1918; Theodore Roosevelt (1901) died on January 6, 1919; and Levi P. Morton (1889–93) died on May 16, 1920.

Three other Presidential Administrations (each of which was only four years long) saw the deaths of three Vice Presidents each:

3 (tie). JOHN QUINCY ADAMS was President from 1825 to 1829. Daniel D. Tompkins (1817–25) died on June 11, 1825; John Adams (1789–97, John Quincy's father) and Thomas Jefferson (1797–1801) both died on July 4, 1826.

3 (tie). ABRAHAM LINCOLN was President from 1861 to 1865. John Tyler (1841) died on January 18, 1862; Martin Van Buren (1833–37) died on July 24, 1862; and George M. Dallas (1845–49) died on December 31, 1864.

3 (tie). GROVER CLEVELAND'S first Administration ran from 1885 to 1889. Thomas A. Hendricks (Cleveland's first Vice President) died in office on November 25, 1885; Chester A. Arthur (1881) died on November 18, 1886; and William A. Wheeler (1877–81) died on June 4, 1887. There were no Vice Presidential deaths during Cleveland's second Administration (1893–97).

THE VICE PRESIDENTS: HOME AND FAMILY

22. *The Five Vice Presidents Who Had the Most Children*

The 47 men who have served as Vice President were even more prolific than the Presidents they served. They combined to father 186 children. The average Vice President has 4 children (2.1 sons and 1.9 daughters). Compare this to the 43 Presidents, who combined to have 156 children, for an average of 3.7 children (2.1 sons and 1.6 daughters).

1. The most prolific Vice President was also the most prolific President: JOHN TYLER. He was Vice President for one month in 1841, after his first eight children were born. He succeeded to the Presidency, and then his wife died in 1842. In 1844, he married again, and after leaving the Presidency, fathered another seven children.

2 (tie). ELBRIDGE GERRY (1813–14) married Ann Thompson in 1786. The following year, they had their first child, and by 1801, they had 10 children.

2 (tie). JOHN C. CALHOUN (1825–32) was almost 29 when he married Floride Bonneau Colhoun, his first cousin once removed (who was almost

19), in January 1811. They had 10 children, the last of whom was born in 1829, while Calhoun was Vice President. Floride outlived John by 16 years.

4 (tie). DANIEL D. TOMPKINS (1817–25) was 24 when he married 16-year-old Hannah Minthorne in early 1798. Their first child wasn't born until 1800, but their eighth, and last, came in 1814. Tompkins died months after leaving the Vice Presidency, in 1825; Hannah survived only until 1829.

4 (tie). GEORGE DALLAS (1845–49) married Sophia Chew Nicklin in 1816, and they had eight children before he became Vice President.

Almosts: HANNIBAL HAMLIN (1861–65) and NELSON ROCKEFELLER (1974–77) each had seven children with two wives. They both had five children with their first wives and two with their second wives. Hamlin had four sons and one daughter with his first wife, Sarah Jane Emery, who died seven years after giving birth the last time. A year and a half later, he married her half-sister, Ellen Vesta Emery, and they had two sons. Rockefeller had three sons and two daughters with his first wife, Mary Todhunter Clark (they divorced when the youngest was 24). The next year, he married Margaretta "Happy" Large Fitler Murphy, another divorcée, and they had two sons.

23. The Five Vice Presidents Who Had the Fewest Children

Though many Vice Presidents were quite prolific, three of them had no children at all, and a further five fathered one each.

WILLIAM R.D. KING (1853), WILLIAM WHEELER (1877–81), and THOMAS MARSHALL (1913–21) all died childless. King was the only Vice President to never marry. Wheeler married Mary King at the age of 26 (she was 17) and remained married to her until her death at the age of 48 (he died 11 years later). The 42-year-old Marshall married 22-year-old Lois Irene Kimsey in 1895; he died in 1925; she outlived him by 33 years.

Five Vice Presidents had one child each:

SCHUYLER COLFAX (1869–73) married Evelyn Clark in 1844. She died childless in 1863. Two weeks after being elected Vice President, Colfax married Ella M. Wade, and in 1870, she gave birth to Schuyler Colfax III.

HENRY WILSON (1873–75) married Harriet Malvina Howe in 1840 (she was 12 years younger than he). They had one son, and then she died in 1870. He died in office.

THOMAS HENDRICKS (1885) married Eliza C. Morton in 1845. Their one son, Morgan, was born in 1848, but he died in 1851. Hendricks died in office, and Eliza survived until 1903.

JOHN NANCE GARNER (1933–41) married Mariette Rheiner when he was 27 and she 26, in 1895. The next year, they had a son, Tully Charles, who outlived his mother by 20 years and his father by one.

HARRY S TRUMAN (1945) married Bess in 1919. Five years later, their only daughter, Mary Margaret, was born. She was a well-known mystery writer who died in 2008.

24. The Five Vice Presidents Who Were the Most Older Than Their Wives, and the Five Vice Presidents Who Were the Most Older Than Their Second Wives

Some Vice Presidents were much older than their wives, either because they married late in life, or because they found very young brides. Others were closer in age. The average Vice President's first (or only) wife was four years, 148 days younger than he was (for Presidents, it was four years, 108 days). Counting all wives, both first marriages and second, the average Vice President was seven years, 158 days older than his wife (for Presidents, it was five years, 316 days). Those Vice Presidents who were the most years older than their first wives include:

1. THOMAS R. MARSHALL (1913–21) was born March 14, 1854, and he was 19 years, 56 days older than his wife, Lois Irene Kimsey (born May 9, 1873). Thomas was an attorney who lost his first run for political office in 1880, but met and fell in love with a woman named Kate Hooper during that campaign. They planned to marry, but she died in 1882, days before the wedding. In 1895, soon after the deaths of his parents (with whom he lived), he met Lois, who was working in her father's law firm. They fell in love and married on October 2, 1895. They spent only two nights apart during their 32 years of marriage.

2. ELBRIDGE GERRY (1813–14) was born July 17, 1744. In the 1785, he was serving in the Congress of the Confederation in New York City when he met Ann Thompson, who was 19 years, 26 days younger than he (she was born August 12, 1763). They married on January 12, 1786, and had 10 children in the next 15 years. In March 1813, Elbridge became the fifth Vice

President, and Ann became the second Second Lady (Gerry's predecessors Thomas Jefferson, Aaron Burr, and George Clinton were all widowers during their terms as Vice President). Their marriage ended November 23, 1814, when Elbridge became the second Vice President to die in office.

3. HENRY WILSON (1873–75) was born February 16, 1812, and was indentured to a farmer as a child. Later, he worked for a shoemaker, learned the trade, and worked as a teacher before starting his own successful shoe manufacturing company. On October 28, 1840, he married Harriet Malvina Howe, who was 12 years, 278 days younger (she was born November 21, 1824). Their one son, Henry Jr. (1846–66) fought during the Civil War. Harriet died in 1870, while Henry was serving in the Senate.

4. LEVI P. MORTON (1889–93) was born May 16, 1824. On October 15, 1856, he married Lucy Young Kimball, who was 12 years, 67 days younger than he (she was born July 22, 1836). He was a merchant and banker during their 15 years of marriage, and they had one child. Lucy died on July 11, 1871, seven years before Levi was elected to his first term in Congress.

5. JOHN C. CALHOUN (1825–32) was born March 18, 1782. On January 8, 1811, he married Floride Bonneau Colhoun, who was nine years, 334 days younger than John (she was born February 15, 1792). Floride's father, John Colhoun, represented South Carolina in the Senate for the last year and a half of his life (he died in 1802) and was a first cousin of her future husband. Two months after John and Floride's marriage, he took his seat in the House of Representatives. Late that year, they had their first child. Their 10th was born in 1829, while John was Vice President.

Ten Vice Presidents remarried (nine after the deaths of their wives, one after divorce). In most of these cases, their second wives were much younger than they. The average Vice President who married twice was 18 years, 341 days older than his second wife (for remarrying Presidents, it was 16 years, 217 days). The greatest age gaps were:

1. ALBEN BARKLEY (1949–53). His first wife, Dorothy, died in 1947, while he was Senate Minority Leader. In 1948, he was elected Vice President on Harry Truman's ticket. And on November 18, 1949, he became the only Vice President to marry while in office. His second wife, Elizabeth Jane Rucker Hadley (known as Jane Rucker Barkley), was 33 years, 303 days younger than he was (he was born on November 24, 1877, she on September 23, 1911). She, too, was a widow. After his Vice Presidency, Alben was reelected to the Senate. He died in 1956, in office, and Jane survived him by eight years.

2. JOHN TYLER (1841–45). His first wife, Letitia, died in 1842, during his only term as President. On June 26, 1844, he married Julia Gardiner, who had been born on May 4, 1820. His new wife was 30 years, 36 days younger than he was, and younger than his three oldest children. She outlived him by more than 27 years, dying in 1889. The Tylers are number one on this list among the Presidents.

3. HANNIBAL HAMLIN (1861–65). His first wife, Sarah Jane Emery, died at the age of 39, in 1855, while Hannibal was a Senator representing Maine. A year and a half after her death, he married her 20-years-younger half-sister, Ellen Vesta Emery, who had been born September 14, 1835, and was 26 years, 18 days younger than her new husband. Hannibal had four children with Sarah and two with Ellen. His first marriage lasted 21 years and his second, almost 35 (until his death in 1891). Ellen survived him by 33 years.

4. LEVI MORTON (1889–93) is the only Vice President or President to appear on both halves of this list (significantly older than his first wife and his second). After his first wife, Lucy, died in 1871, he married Anna Livingston Reade Street on February 12, 1873. Born May 18, 1846, she was born two days after Levi's 22nd birthday. They had five daughters in the next decade, and Levi served in the House of Representatives, as Minister to France, as Governor of New York, and as the 22nd Vice President. Levi

outlived Anna, too (she died in August 1918, he on his 96th birthday, in May 1920).

5. AARON BURR (1801–05). The third Vice President was the first to be dropped from his President's reelection ticket and the first to remarry. His first wife died in 1794, while he was a Senator. After his 1807 trial (and acquittal) for treason, he fled the country and lived in Europe for several years. After returning to the US, he lived quietly. On July 1, 1833, he married Eliza Bowen Jumel, a wealthy widow 19 years, 60 days younger than he (she was born on April 2, 1775). They separated after months of marriage, when she realized he was squandering her fortune on failed land speculation. Their divorce was finalized September 14, 1836, the day of his death.

25. The Five Vice Presidents Who Were the Most Younger Than Their Wives

Six Vice Presidents of the 46 Vice Presidents who married chose wives who were older than they were (as did six of the 41 married Presidents). In fact, the average Vice President's first (or only) wife was four years, 148 days younger than he was. Counting all wives, both first marriages and second, the average Vice President was seven years, 158 days older than his wife. Those Vice Presidents who were younger than their wives were:

1. AARON BURR (1801–05). The exact date (even the year) of birth of his first wife, Theodosia Bartow Prevost, is not precisely known. What is known is that Theodosia was a widow with five children when she married Aaron on July 2, 1782. She was 8–10 years older than her new husband. Aaron and Theodosia had two children during their marriage, though only one, daughter Theodosia, survived to adulthood. Theodosia Bartow Prevost Burr died of stomach cancer on May 28, 1794. The younger Theodosia married Joseph Alston in 1801. They had one son, who died in 1812 at the age of 10. Later that year, Alston became Governor of South Carolina. In January 1813, Theodosia Burr Alston was lost at sea when the schooner aboard which she was sailing, the *Patriot*, disappeared.

2. MILLARD FILLMORE (1850–53). In early 1826, lawyer Millard Fillmore married Abigail Powers, who was one year, 296 days older than he was (she was born on March 17, 1798, he on January 7, 1800). She had two children and, as First Lady, pushed Congress into funding the White House's first permanent library. She died less than a month after her husband left office, having caught cold at his successor's inauguration. Fillmore remarried five years later. (Millard and Abigail Fillmore are also #2 on the Presidential version of this list.)

3. NELSON ROCKEFELLER (1974–77). On June 23, 1930, Nelson A. Rockefeller married Mary Todhunter Clark. Nelson was the third child (second son) of John D. Rockefeller, Jr., who was the only son of John D. Rockefeller, founder of Standard Oil and the family fortune. Nelson was born on July 8, 1908; Mary on June 17, 1907 (she was one year, 21 days older than he). They had five children between 1932 and 1938 (the last two were twins). In 1958, Nelson was elected the 49th Governor of New York. On March 16, 1962, Mary ended her tenure as First Lady of New York, when the Rockefellers' divorce was finalized. He was appointed Vice President in 1974, and died in January 1979. She died in April 1999.

4. RICHARD NIXON (1969–74). Nixon married Thelma Catherine "Pat" Ryan in 1940. She was 299 days older than he, having been born on March 16, 1912. They remained married through his Vice Presidency, electoral defeat in 1960, and election to and then resignation from the Presidency, until her death in 1993. He died 304 days later, on April 22, 1994. (Richard and Pat Nixon are also #4 on the Presidential version of this list.)

5. HENRY A. WALLACE (1941–45). On May 20, 1914, newspaperman and farmer Henry A. Wallace married Monmouth College graduate Ilo Browne. She was 211 days older than he (she was born March 10, and he October 7, 1888). In the next six years, they would have three children (who would all live into the twenty-first century). In 1921, Henry's father, Henry C. Wallace, was appointed the seventh Secretary of Agriculture. In 1926, Henry A. and Ilo (with the help of her inheritance) founded the Hi-Bred Corn Company, which is now known as Pioneer Hi-Bred International and is the world's second-largest seed company. In 1933, Henry A. followed his father, when he was appointed the 11th Secretary of Agriculture. After his one term as Vice President, he was the 10th Secretary of Commerce. Henry died in November 1965, Ilo in February 1981.

26. The Five Vice Presidents Who Predeceased Their Wives by the Longest Time

Some Vice Presidents died long before their wives, but not all of them died in office. Of the 40 sets of Vice Presidents and first wives who are both deceased, 19 wives outlived their husbands (and 21 husbands outlived their wives). [Among Presidents, the wives tend to be longer-lived, in 20 of 35 cases.] On average, the wives outlived their husbands by 18 years, 221 days (compared to a scant two years, 309 days for Presidential wives). Factoring in the eight second wives who outlived their Vice President-husbands, the average becomes 20 years, 154 days (for Presidents, it's six years, 82 days).

1. GARRET A. HOBART (1897–99) died in office on November 21, 1899, aged 55. His wife, Esther Jane, who was five years younger, survived him by more than 41 years, dying on January 8, 1941. She outlived only four of her successors, but lived to see eight more men become Vice President.

2. LYNDON BAINES JOHNSON (1961–63) succeeded to the Presidency when John Kennedy was assassinated, then was elected to his own term in 1964, and died four years after retiring from the Presidency, on January 22, 1973, before his 65th birthday. His widow, Claudia Alta "Lady Bird" Taylor, died at the age of 94, on July 11, 2007. She survived her husband by 34 years, 170 days. (The Johnsons are #4 on this list among Presidents.)

3. ELBRIDGE GERRY (1813–14) was the second Vice President to die in office. He is also #2 on the list of Vice Presidents who were significantly older than their wives. He was 19 years, 26 days older than Ann Thompson, his wife, and following his death, she survived him by another 34 years, 114 days.

4. THOMAS R. MARSHALL (1913–21) is also on the list of Vice Presidents who were much older than their wives. In fact, he's number one on that list: he was 19 years, 56 days older than his wife, Lois Irene Kimsey. Thomas died four years after leaving office, on June 1, 1925. Lois survived another 32 years, 220 days, dying January 6, 1958.

5. JOHN C. BRECKINRIDGE (1857–61) lived his life very early. He joined the House of Representatives at the age of 30 and then was the youngest Vice President (took office at the age of 36). After those four years, he joined the Senate, but a few months later joined the Confederate Army. He was indicted for treason and expelled from the Senate. Late in the Civil War, he was named the fifth Secretary of War of the CSA and, after the war, fled the country. He returned to the USA in 1868, and died in May 1875, at the age of 54 (he is #2 on the list of the Vice Presidents who died the youngest). His wife, Mary Cyrene Burch, was five years younger than John. She survived him by 32 years, 144 days, dying on October 8, 1907.

Eight of the Vice Presidents' second wives have outlived them, by an average of 24 years, 267 days (compared to the Presidents' second wives, who outlived their husbands by an average of 29 years, 318 days). The Vice Presidents whose second wives were widows the longest are:

1. NELSON ROCKEFELLER (1974–77) died two years after leaving office, on January 26, 1979. He is the only deceased Vice President to be survived by two wives: he and Mary Todhunter Clark had divorced in 1962; she died in 1999. His second wife, Margaretta Large Fitler Murphy "Happy" Rockefeller, who was 18 years younger than he, died on May 19, 2015, a widow for 36 years, 113 days.

2. HANNIBAL HAMLIN (1861–65) was dropped from Abraham Lincoln's ticket for the reelection campaign of 1864, but he outlived Lincoln by 26 years, dying on July 4, 1891. His second wife, Ellen Vesta Emery (half-sister of his deceased first wife), was 26 years younger than he (they appear

on the list of Vice Presidents significantly older than their wives). Ellen died on February 1, 1925, having survived Hannibal by 33 years, 212 days.

3. THEODORE ROOSEVELT (1901–09) lost his first wife after less than three years of marriage, in 1884. He married Edith Kermit Carow in 1886, and together they had five more children. He was Vice President for six months in 1901, before William McKinley was assassinated. Theodore retired from the Presidency in 1909, and then attempted to come back in the election of 1912, but lost to Woodrow Wilson. He died on January 6, 1919. Edith, a scant three years younger than her husband, outlived him by 29 years, 268 days, dying on September 30, 1948. (They are also #3 on this list among Presidents.)

4. AARON BURR (1801–05) had been retired from the Vice Presidency for 28 years (and widowed for 39 years) when he married wealthy widow Eliza Bowen Jumel on July 1, 1833 (she was 19 years younger than he). Their marriage was brief; they separated during their first year of marriage, when she discovered he was squandering her fortune on failed investments. Their divorce was finalized, ironically, on the day of his death, September 14, 1836. She survived him by 28 years, 305 days, dying on July 16, 1865.

5. JOHN TYLER (1841–45) was Vice President for one month before becoming the first to succeed to the Presidency upon his successor's death. He became a widower while serving as President, as his first wife, Letitia Christian, died on September 10, 1842. On June 26, 1844, he became the first President to marry when he married Julia Gardiner, who was 30 years younger than he (and younger than his three oldest children). After leaving the White House, John and Julia had seven children. The last, Pearl, was born in 1860, when Tyler was 70 years old. He died before Pearl's second birthday, on January 18, 1862. Julia outlived him by 27 years, 173 days, dying on July 10, 1889. (They are #4 on this list among Presidents.)

27. The Five Vice Presidents Who Outlived Their Wives by the Longest Time

More than half the Vice Presidents outlived their first wives: 21 of 40 (as opposed to 15 of the 35 Presidents). Those 21 Vice Presidents outlived their first wives by an average of 19 years, 328 days. Those who lived the longest without their wives are:

1. LEVI MORTON (1889–93) was 32, 12 years older than his first wife, Lucy Young Kimball, when they married in October 1856. She died 11 days before her 35th birthday, in 1871. At the time, he was a businessman and banker, still eight years away from holding his first elected office. When he died on his 96th birthday, in May 1920, he had been widowed 48 years, 309 days.

Morton is unique among Vice Presidents (or Presidents, for that matter) in that he also outlived his second wife. Nearly two years after Lucy's death, he married Anna Livingston Reade Street, on February 12, 1873. Anna was 22 years younger than Levi and bore him five daughters in the next decade. She was Second Lady during his Vice Presidency, and she died at the age of 72, on August 14, 1918. Levi outlived her by one year, 275 days.

2. THOMAS JEFFERSON (1797–1801). Jefferson and 23-year-old widow Martha Wayles Skelton were married on January 1, 1772. They had six children—two of whom lived to adulthood—before she died on September 6, 1782. Jefferson never remarried and outlived his wife by 43 years, 304 days, dying on July 4, 1826. Jefferson was the first of three Vice Presidents in a row to be widowers. (Jefferson is #1 on this list among Presidents.)

3. MARTIN VAN BUREN (1833–37) married Hannah Hoes, his first cousin once removed, on February 21, 1807. They had five children—four of whom lived to adulthood—before she died on February 5, 1819. Van Buren

never remarried and outlived his wife by 43 years, 169 days, dying on July 24, 1862. (Van Buren is #2 on this list among Presidents.)

4. AARON BURR (1801–05) married Theodosia Bartow Prevost, a widow significantly older than he was, with five children, in 1782. They had two children, though only one—daughter Theodosia—survived to adulthood. Aaron's wife Theodosia died of stomach cancer on May 28, 1794, while he was serving in the Senate. Aaron died 42 years, 109 days after his first wife, on September 14, 1836.

5. HANNIBAL HAMLIN (1861–65) was six years older than his first wife, Sarah Jane Emery. They married in 1833, and had four children. She died in 1855, aged 39. The next year, he married her half-sister, Ellen. When he died, on July 4, 1891, Sarah had been dead for 36 years, 78 days.

28. The Ten Vice Presidents Who Had More Than One Wife

Six of the 43 Presidents were married twice (five were widowed and one, Ronald Reagan, was divorced). Ten of the 47 Vice Presidents were married twice. One, William R.D. King, was never married. And of the 36 who were married once, Richard Mentor Johnson was not officially married, but had a common law wife, Julia Chinn, a slave left to him by his father (they had two children).

1. AARON BURR (1801–05) married Theodosia Bartow Prevost in 1782 (she was a widow at the time). They had one daughter, also named Theodosia, before she died in 1794. Much later in life, in 1833, Burr married Eliza Bowen Jumel, but that marriage didn't last long. Indeed, their divorce was finalized the day of his death, September 14, 1836.

2. JOHN TYLER (1841) married Letitia Christian in 1813. They had eight children before Tyler was elected Vice President. After William Henry Harrison's death, Tyler became the first Vice President to succeed to the Presidency, in 1841. In 1842, Letitia became the first First Lady to die while her husband was President. And in 1844, he became the first President to marry while in office, when he married Julia Gardiner (she was 30 years younger than he). After he retired from the Presidency, they had seven children.

3. MILLARD FILLMORE (1849–50) married Abigail Powers in 1826. They had two children and were together through his Vice Presidency and Presidency (he, too, succeeded to the office upon the death of his President). Abigail caught a cold at his successor's inaugural festivities and died a month after moving out of the White House. In 1858, he married widow Caroline Carmichael McIntosh, who was 13 years younger than he.

4. HANNIBAL HAMLIN (1861–65) married Sarah Jane Emery in 1833 (she was 18; he was 24). They had five children (including two sons who served as Generals during the Civil War), before she died of tuberculosis in 1855. The next year, he married his first wife's half-sister, Ellen Vesta Emery, with whom he had two more children.

5. SCHUYLER COLFAX (1869–73) married Evelyn Clark in 1844. They had no children before her death in 1863. On November 18, 1868, two weeks after Colfax was elected Vice President, he married Ella M. Wade. In 1870, they had a son, Schuyler Colfax III.

6. LEVI P. MORTON (1889–93) married Lucy Young Kimball in 1856 (she was 24, he 32), and they had one child. She died in 1871, and two years later—when he was 49 and she was 27—he married Anna Livingston Reade Street, with whom he had five daughters.

7. THEODORE ROOSEVELT (1901) married Alice Hathaway Lee in 1880. She died in 1884, two days after giving birth to their only daughter, also named Alice. In 1886, he married Edith Kermit Carow, who had been a guest at his first wedding. They had five more children in the next 11 years. She outlived him by 29 years.

8. ALBEN W. BARKLEY (1949–53) married Dorothy Brower in 1903, and they had three children. She died in 1947. On November 18, 1949, he became the only Vice President to marry while in office (three Presidents have done so), when he married widow Elizabeth Jane Rucker Hadley, who was known as Jane Hadley Barkley. He died in 1956, she in 1964.

9. NELSON ROCKEFELLER (1974–77) married Mary Todhunter Clark in 1930 (she was 11 months older than he), and they had five children, including Michael Clark in 1938, who disappeared on an expedition in Indonesia in 1961, and is thought to have been killed by cannibals. They divorced in 1962 (Rockefeller is the only Vice President to have been divorced).

In 1963, he married Margaretta "Happy" Fitler Murphy, who was herself divorced with four children. They had two more children in the 1960s.

10. JOE BIDEN (2009–) married Neilia Hunter in 1966. They had three children between 1969 and 1971, but in December 1972, she was in a car accident with her children in the car. She and their youngest child, daughter Naomi Christina, were killed (their two sons were seriously injured, but survived). In 1977, he married Jill Tracy Jacobs, with whom he had a daughter in 1981.

29. The Vice Presidents Who Got Married While in Office

Marriage is usually considered an earlier-in-life event than running for national office, and in modern times, the nearly 24-hour-a-day schedule of the Presidency leaves little time for things like dating, but three of our Presidents did manage to get married while in office. Two of them were widowers who remarried, while the third married for the first time. We've had 47 Vice Presidents, to 43 Presidents, but only one Vice President has married while in office. Another came close.

ALBEN BARKLEY (1945–49) married Dorothy Anne Brower on June 23, 1903. They had three children over the next several years. In 1913, he was elected to the House of Representatives and in 1927, to the Senate. He was Senate Minority Leader from July 1937 to January 4, 1947, when he became Majority Leader. On March 10, 1947, Dorothy died, after suffering from heart disease for a long time. Alben continued in his Senate role. In the summer of 1948, Harry Truman chose him as his Vice Presidential running mate, and in November of that year, they upset challenger Thomas Dewey. At 71, Alben was the oldest man elected Vice President.

On July 8, 1949, he met 37-year-old widow Jane Rucker Hadley at a party thrown by Clark Clifford (at the time, Clifford was White House Counsel). After she returned to St. Louis, they kept in contact with letters and commercial airplane trips. They announced their engagement on October 31, and on November 18, they married in St. John's Methodist Church in St. Louis.

Before meeting Alben, Jane had been an ardent Republican. In 1940, she worked in Republican nominee Wendell Wilkie's St. Louis office. After Alben and Jane's marriage, he was asked about her politics and replied, "She got swept off her feet by Wilkie, but now she's back in the fold."

Alben served one term as Vice President and then was elected to a new term in the Senate in 1954. He died of a heart attack in 1956. After his death, Jane took a job as a secretary at George Washington University and, in 1958, published a memoir called *I Married the Veep*. She died of a heart attack in 1964.

The almost: SCHUYLER COLFAX (1869–73) married Evelyn Clark on October 10, 1844; they had known each other since childhood. In 1855, he was elected to the House of Representatives. On July 10, 1863, Evelyn died, and in December of that year, Schuyler was elected the 25th Speaker of the House. In 1865, as Speaker, he voted for and then announced the passage of the 13th Amendment. In 1868, he was chosen as the Vice Presidential candidate on Ulysses Grant's ticket, and they went on to win the election.

On November 18, 1868, fifteen days after being elected Vice President, Schuyler married Ella M. Wade, who was 13 years younger than he. Ella's uncle, Senator Benjamin Franklin Wade of Ohio, was President pro tempore of the Senate at that time. Schuyler and Ella had one son, Schuyler Colfax III (born 1870), who served as mayor of South Bend, Indiana, from 1898 to 1901.

In 1872, Schuyler was implicated in the Crédit Mobilier scandal, for taking a bribe while he was a Congressman, and he was dropped from Grant's reelection ticket. After leaving office, he was a successful lecturer.

On January 13, 1885, while changing trains in Mankato, Minnesota, Schuyler died of a heart attack, apparently brought on by the extreme cold and exhaustion. Ella died on March 4, 1911.

30. The Vice Presidents Known for Having Facial Hair

As with the Presidents with whom they served, the Vice Presidents known for sporting facial hair were confined to a very limited period of American history. Presidential whiskers were confined to the 48-year span from Abraham Lincoln (1861) to Theodore Roosevelt (1909). Vice Presidents followed suit, but with fewer beards and more mustaches, spanning from 1869 to 1933.

The first Vice President elected with facial hair had only a beard and no mustache: Vice President SCHUYLER COLFAX (1869–73). The only other Vice President to sport a beard was CHARLES FAIRBANKS (1905–09), who wore a bushy mustache with a goatee. (Four Presidents wore full beards with mustaches.)

Six other Vice Presidents wore mustaches without beards. Four Presidents (including two Vice Presidents who succeeded) also favored this style. The mustachioed Vice Presidents were: CHESTER ARTHUR (1881), ADLAI STEVENSON (1893–97), GARRET HOBART (1897–99), THEODORE ROOSEVELT (1901), THOMAS MARSHALL (1913–21), and CHARLES CURTIS (1929–33).

Standing out from the crowd was LEVI MORTON (1889–93), who sported a mustache with truly remarkable muttonchops in the years before he was elected Vice President (though he was clean-shaven for the election of 1888).

THE VICE PRESIDENTS: RESUME

31. The Most Popular Colleges Attended by the Vice Presidents

The most popular colleges Vice Presidents-to-be graduated from are:

1. HARVARD. Four future Vice Presidents graduated from Harvard (two of whom are among the eight Presidents from Harvard): John Adams (graduated in 1755), Elbridge Gerry (1762), Theodore Roosevelt (1880), and Al Gore (1969).

2. YALE. Three future Vice Presidents graduated from Yale (two of whom are among the five Presidents from Yale): John C. Calhoun (1804), Gerald Ford (who graduated from the Law School in 1941), and George H.W. Bush (1948).

3. PRINCETON (which was earlier known as the College of New Jersey) claims two Presidential graduates. Three future Vice Presidents attended the school, but only two of them graduated: Aaron Burr (1772) and George Dallas (1810). John C. Breckinridge attended, but did not receive a degree.

4 (tie). CENTRE COLLEGE IN DANVILLE, KENTUCKY: John C. Breckinridge (1839) and Adlai E. Stevenson (1855).

4 (tie). TRANSYLVANIA UNIVERSITY IN LEXINGTON, KENTUCKY: Richard M. Johnson (1802) and John C. Breckinridge (1840).

4 (tie). THE COLLEGE OF WILLIAM AND MARY: Thomas Jefferson (attended from 1760 to 1762: he did not receive a degree, but did complete his studies) and John Tyler (1807).

4 (tie). THE UNIVERSITY OF MINNESOTA granted two degrees to future Vice Presidents, but they both went to the same man: Walter Mondale received his bachelor's degree in 1951, and his law degree in 1956.

Two other schools had two future Vice Presidents as students, but in each case, only one received a degree:

COLUMBIA: Daniel Tompkins (graduated in 1795) and Theodore Roosevelt (attended the law school, but did not receive a degree).

VANDERBILT: John Nance Garner (did not receive a degree) and Al Gore (graduated from the law school in 1976).

The other colleges that can claim one Vice President each are: the University of North Carolina (King); University of Vermont (Wheeler, did not graduate); Union College (Arthur); Hanover College (Hendricks); Illinois Wesleyan (Stevenson, did not graduate); Rutgers (Hobart); Ohio Wesleyan (Fairbanks); Hamilton College (Sherman); Wabash College (Marshall); Amherst College (Coolidge); Marietta College (Dawes); Cincinnati Law School (Dawes); Emory University (Barkley); University of Virginia School of Law (Barkley); Iowa State College at Ames (Wallace); University of Missouri Kansas City School of Law (Truman, did not graduate); Whittier College (Nixon); Duke University School of Law (Nixon); Southwest Texas State Teachers College (LBJohnson); Capitol

College of Pharmacy in Denver, Colorado (Humphrey); Louisiana State University (Humphrey); Johns Hopkins (Agnew); University of Baltimore Law School (Agnew); University of Michigan (Ford); Dartmouth College (Rockefeller); DePauw University (Quayle); Indiana University School of Law University (Quayle); University of Wyoming (Cheney); University of Delaware (Biden); and Syracuse University College of Law (Biden).

32. *The Vice Presidents Who Did Not Attend College or Did Not Receive Degrees*

Nine Vice Presidents did not attend college (although several of them did study law under lawyers before being admitted to the bar, at a time before there were law schools):

1. George Clinton enlisted in the British army to fight in the French and Indian War at the age of 18 (in 1757). He rose to the rank of Lieutenant, and then he studied law and was admitted to the bar at about the age of 20. His political career began in 1759, when he was appointed County Clerk for Ulster County, New York (he held that position until his death). His first elected office was as a member of the New York Provincial Assembly, representing Ulster County, starting in 1768, and he was first elected Governor of New York in 1777.

2. Martin Van Buren began studying law under local lawyer Francis Sylvester at the age of 14 in his native Kinderhook, New York. He worked for Sylvester for six years (summing up a routine case before a jury at age 15). He moved to New York City for another year of apprenticeship, to William P. Van Ness, and then was admitted to the New York bar in 1803.

3. Millard Fillmore worked for and studied under county judge Walter Wood in Montville, New York, for two years. He left in 1821, following a dispute with the judge, and returned home. The following year, he continued his studies under Asa Rice and Joseph Clary, and then was admitted to the New York bar in 1823.

4. Hannibal Hamlin attended Hebron Academy (a college prep school), but then returned home to take charge of the family farm. He worked as a surveyor, in a printing office, and as a school teacher while studying law.

He was admitted to the bar in 1833 and practiced in his native Maine until 1848 (when he was elected to the Senate).

5. ANDREW JOHNSON had absolutely no formal education. He taught himself to read as an adult while he was apprenticed to a tailor as a teenager. Later, while he was running his own tailoring shop in Tennessee, his wife helped him improve his education by reading to him. When he was 22, he was elected Mayor of Greeneville, Tennessee.

6. SCHUYLER COLFAX attended school into his teenage years, but didn't go on to college. At the age of 18, he was appointed Deputy Auditor of St. Joseph County (Indiana) and started writing for the *Indiana State Journal* and *New York Tribune*. At the age of 19, he became the editor of the *South Bend Free Press*, which he bought three years later, changing the name to the *St. Joseph Valley Register*. He was a member of the Indiana Constitutional Convention in 1850, and an unsuccessful candidate for the House of Representatives the same year. He was first elected to the House in 1854.

7. HENRY WILSON attended public school and several local pre-college academies in Massachusetts, but did not attend college. He was a shoe-maker at the age of 21 and also taught school. He was first elected to the state legislature at the age of 29.

8. LEVI MORTON attended public schools and Shoreham Academy in Vermont, but left school early and was a clerk in a general store in Massachusetts when he was 14. A few years later, he was a teacher in New Hampshire and then a merchant, before moving to Boston at the age of 26 and then to New York City four years later, where he went into banking. He ran unsuccessfully for the House of Representatives in 1876, and was elected in 1878.

9. CHARLES CURTIS graduated from Topeka (Kansas) High School and then studied law. He was admitted to the bar in 1881, and practiced in Topeka.

He was the Shawnee County Prosecuting Attorney from 1885 to 1889. He was first elected to the House of Representatives in 1892.

In addition, three Vice Presidents attended college, but did not graduate.

1. WILLIAM WHEELER attended the University of Vermont, but was forced to drop out because of monetary concerns. He later studied law and was admitted to the bar in 1845.

2. JOHN NANCE GARNER attended Vanderbilt University, but dropped out after only one semester. He returned home, studied law, and was admitted to the bar in 1890.

3. HARRY TRUMAN graduated from Independence High School in 1901, but was unable to apply to West Point because of bad eyesight. Finances kept him from attending another college. After serving in World War I, he studied at Kansas City Law School (which is now the University of Missouri-Kansas City School of Law) for two years in the early 1920s, but did not receive a degree. He is the last President who did not earn a college degree.

33. The Most Popular Pre-Vice Presidential Jobs

More than half (22 of 43) of the Presidents were lawyers before they became President, but that percentage is dwarfed by would-be Vice Presidents, of whom 33 were lawyers. And while a majority of the Presidents (29) served in the military (though it wasn't a career for most of them), fewer Vice Presidents (20) had military experience.

LAWYER: The lawyers who became Vice President were: Adams, Jefferson, Burr, Clinton, Tompkins, Calhoun, Van Buren, RMJohnson, Tyler, Dallas, Fillmore, King, Breckinridge, Hamlin, Wheeler, Arthur, Hendricks, Stevenson, Hobart, Fairbanks, Sherman, Marshall, Coolidge, Dawes, Curtis, Garner, Barkley, Nixon, Agnew, Ford, Mondale, Quayle, and Biden.

REPRESENTATIVE: Among Presidents, an equal number were lawyers and state legislators. Among Vice Presidents, however, the second-most popular job was serving as a member of the House of Representatives (18 Representatives later became President, putting this job fourth on their list). The 25 Representatives who became Vice Presidents were: Gerry, Calhoun, RMJohnson, Tyler, Fillmore, King, Breckinridge, Hamlin, AJohnson, Colfax, Wheeler, Hendricks, Morton, Stevenson, Sherman, Curtis, Garner, Barkley, Nixon, LBJohnson, Ford, Bush, Quayle, Gore, and Cheney. Four each represented districts in Indiana and New York, three each were from Kentucky and Texas, and two from Tennessee. The other states that had future Vice Presidents represent them in the House of Representatives were: California, Kansas, Massachusetts, Maine, Michigan, North Carolina, South Carolina, Virginia, and Wyoming.

In addition, two of the Representatives had served as Speaker of the House, making them the only two people to be the presiding officer of both houses of Congress: Schuyler Colfax (1863–69) and John Nance Garner (1931–33). Only one Speaker, James Knox Polk (1835–39), became President.

Daniel Tompkins was elected to the House from New York, but did not take his seat, opting instead to accept appointment to the New York State Supreme Court.

SENATOR: Only 15 Senators became President (this job ranks fifth on that list), but 23 Senators moved on to the Vice Presidency. The Senators who were later elected Vice President include: Burr, Calhoun, Van Buren, RMJohnson, Tyler, Dallas, King, Breckinridge, Hamlin, AJohnson, HWilson, Hendricks, Fairbanks, Curtis, Truman, Barkley, Nixon, LBJohnson, Humphrey, Mondale, Quayle, Gore, and Biden. Three represented Indiana; two each were from Kentucky, Minnesota, New York, and Tennessee. The other states that had future Vice Presidents representing them in the Senate were Alabama, California, Delaware, Kansas, Massachusetts, Maine, Missouri, Pennsylvania, South Carolina, Texas, and Virginia.

Breckinridge is the only Vice President who later served in the Senate, representing Kentucky, but three Senators moved to the Vice Presidency and then back to the Senate: Calhoun, Hamlin, and Humphrey.

Three future Vice Presidents served as President pro tempore of the Senate: Tyler, King, and Curtis. And one former Vice President, Humphrey, was named Deputy President pro tempore.

STATE LEGISLATOR: Only 16 Vice Presidents had previously served as state legislators, compared to 22 Presidents. The Vice Presidents were: Burr, Clinton, Tompkins, Van Buren, RMJohnson, Tyler, Fillmore, Breckinridge, Hamlin, AJohnson, HWilson, Wheeler, Hendricks, Hobart, Coolidge, and Garner. Six served in New York, two each in Kentucky and Massachusetts.

LOCAL GOVERNMENT: Fifteen future Vice Presidents served in their local governments at various levels, from Mayor to District Attorney to Judge: Dallas, AJohnson, Wheeler, Stevenson, Hobart, TRoosevelt, Sherman, Coolidge, Curtis, Garner, Truman, Barkley, Humphrey, Agnew, and Biden.

GOVERNOR: Fourteen future Vice Presidents served as Governors (the 19 Governors who became President ranks that job third on the Presidential list): Jefferson, Clinton, Gerry, Tompkins, Van Buren, Tyler, Hamlin, AJohnson, Hendricks, TRoosevelt, Marshall, Coolidge, Agnew, and Rockefeller. Five of them were Governor of New York; two each of Indiana, Massachusetts, and Virginia; and one each of Maryland, Maine, and Tennessee. In addition, Morton is the only one to become a Governor after his Vice Presidency, also of New York.

BUSINESSMAN/ENTREPRENEUR: Ten future Vice Presidents were businessmen of some sort: Gerry, RMJohnson, Morton, Hobart, Fairbanks, Sherman, Wallace, Rockefeller, Bush, and Cheney.

OTHER JOBS: Other shared pre-Vice Presidential jobs include: Federal government positions below Cabinet level (eight future Vice Presidents served in the Federal government); landowner/farmer/rancher (eight); Ambassador (seven men served as Ambassadors before becoming Vice President, and four retired Vice Presidents served as Ambassadors); Cabinet Secretaries (seven); newspaper writer/editor/owner (seven); teacher (seven); tradesman (four); member of the Continental Congress (three); banker (three); and shopkeeper (three).

34. The Vice Presidents Who Served in the Government after Their Terms of Office

This list does not include those Vice Presidents who went on to be President (John Tyler and Andrew Johnson) and then held other posts after their Presidencies. In total, six Presidents had post-Presidential government jobs: John Quincy Adams, John Tyler, Andrew Johnson, Ulysses Grant, William Howard Taft, and Dwight Eisenhower. Among them were one Representative, one Senator, and one Chief Justice.

The 10 former Vice Presidents who later served in other posts include:

1. JOHN C. CALHOUN. The seventh Vice President (1825–32), and the first to resign, he left office to take the seat he'd just been elected to in the Senate, representing South Carolina. After his Vice Presidency, he was in the Senate from December 29, 1832, to March 3, 1843, and then again from November 26, 1845, to March 31, 1850 (the day he died). In between, he was the 16th US Secretary of State, serving under John Tyler and (briefly) James Knox Polk from April 1, 1844, to March 10, 1845.

2. GEORGE M. DALLAS. The 11th Vice President (1845–49) was appointed Envoy Extraordinary and Minister Plenipotentiary (aka Ambassador) to Britain by Franklin Pierce. He served from 1856 to 1861.

3. JOHN C. BRECKINRIDGE. The 14th Vice President (1857–61), and youngest ever, moved from the Vice Presidency to the Senate seat Kentucky had elected him to, but served in that body only briefly, from March 4 to December 4, 1861. He was expelled by resolution for supporting the South. Later, he was the fifth Secretary of War of the Confederacy, serving from February 6 to May 10, 1865.

4. HANNIBAL HAMLIN. The 15th Vice President (1861–65) was dropped from Lincoln's reelection ticket in favor of southern Democrat Andrew Johnson, who had remained loyal to the Union. Late in his Vice Presidency, Hamlin served for a brief time with the Maine Coast Guard in 1864. After leaving office, he was elected to the Senate, representing Maine, from March 4, 1869, to March 3, 1881. In January 1881, President James Garfield appointed him Envoy Extraordinary and Minister Plenipotentiary (aka Ambassador) to Spain, where he served from December 20, 1881, to October 17, 1882.

5. LEVI P. MORTON. The 22nd Vice President (1889–93) was elected the 31st Governor of New York, serving one term, from January 1, 1895, to December 31, 1896.

6. CHARLES G. DAWES. The 30th Vice President (1925–29) was appointed Ambassador to Great Britain by President Herbert Hoover and served from 1929 to 1932. Dawes left Britain when Hoover appointed him Chairman of the Reconstruction Finance Corporation, where he served for less than a year.

7. HENRY A. WALLACE. The 33rd Vice President (1941–45) had been President Franklin Roosevelt's Secretary of Agriculture when he was chosen to replace John Nance Garner as Vice President for Roosevelt's third term. For his fourth term, however, the Democratic Party was uncomfortable with the possibility that Wallace might succeed Roosevelt as President and forced his removal from the ticket. Roosevelt instead appointed Wallace the 10th Secretary of Commerce. Wallace served from March 2, 1945, until September 20, 1946, when President Harry Truman fired him.

8. ALBEN W. BARKLEY. The 35th Vice President (1949–53) was elected by Kentucky to the US Senate, where he took his seat on January 3, 1955. He died in office on April 30, 1956.

9. HUBERT HORATIO HUMPHREY, JR. The 38th Vice President (1965–69) unsuccessfully ran for the Presidency in 1968. In 1970, he was elected to the US Senate by Minnesota and served there from January 3, 1971, to January 13, 1978. He died in office, and his wife, Muriel, was appointed to fill his seat. She served less than a year, until she was replaced in the special election. Muriel Humphrey was the only Vice Presidential wife to hold public office.

10. WALTER F. MONDALE. The 42nd Vice President (1977–81) lost the Presidential election of 1984 to Republican Ronald Reagan. The next Democratic President, Bill Clinton, appointed Mondale the 24th US Ambassador to Japan, and Mondale served in that post from September 21, 1993, to December 15, 1996.

35. The Vice Presidents Who Were Elected President

1. JOHN ADAMS. The first Vice President (1789–97) ran for the Presidency when George Washington announced he would not seek a third term. In the election of 1796, Adams won 71 of the electoral votes to Thomas Jefferson's 68, making Adams the second President and Jefferson the second Vice President (in the first four elections, the candidate receiving the second-greatest number of electoral votes became Vice President).

2. THOMAS JEFFERSON. The second Vice President (1797–1801) ran against the sitting President in the election of 1800, Jefferson as a Democrat-Republican, Adams as a Federalist. Jefferson received 73 electoral votes to Adams's 65, but Aaron Burr, Jefferson's Vice Presidential candidate, also received 73 electoral votes. Because of the tie, it was up to the House of Representatives to decide the winner. The House took 36 ballots between February 11 and February 17, 1801, before finally choosing Jefferson. This deadlock and debate prompted the passage of the 12th Amendment, providing for the election of the President and Vice President as a ticket. Jefferson and his new Vice Presidential candidate, George Clinton, won the election of 1804, defeating Charles Pinckney (who had run as Adams's Vice Presidential candidate in 1800).

3. MARTIN VAN BUREN. After serving as Andrew Jackson's first Secretary of State, he replaced Vice President John C. Calhoun on the ticket in 1832, for Jackson's second term, and served as Vice President from 1833 to 1837. In 1837, Van Buren became the first sitting Vice President since Thomas Jefferson to run for the Presidency and the last to win it until George H.W. Bush in 1988. Van Buren received 170 electoral votes, to William Henry Harrison's 73. Harrison would come back to defeat Van Buren

in the election of 1840. Van Buren made another comeback, running for President on the Free Soil ticket in 1848. He failed to win any electoral votes, but took enough of the popular vote (10 percent) to tip the election to Zachary Taylor from Lewis Cass.

4. THEODORE ROOSEVELT. After Vice President Garret Hobart died in office in 1899, Theodore Roosevelt was nominated for the spot when President William McKinley ran for reelection in 1900. Following McKinley's assassination in September 1901, Roosevelt became the youngest President ever (he was 42 years, 322 days old when he was inaugurated on September 14, 1901). In the election of 1904, Roosevelt was elected to his own term as President, winning 336 electoral votes to 140 for fellow New Yorker Democrat Alton Parker.

Roosevelt was the first Vice President to succeed to the Presidency and then be elected in his own right. John Tyler succeeded William Henry Harrison in 1841, but wasn't nominated for his own term in 1844. Millard Fillmore succeeded Zachary Taylor in 1850, wasn't nominated in 1852, but did run on a third-party ticket in 1856, coming in third to James Buchanan and John C. Frémont. Andrew Johnson succeeded upon Abraham Lincoln's assassination in 1865, but after his impeachment (and acquittal), he wasn't nominated for his own term. Chester Arthur succeeded upon James Garfield's death, but he, too, was unable to win nomination for his own term.

During the 1904 campaign, Roosevelt pledged not to seek another term in 1908. He did, however, come back in 1912 to challenge William Howard Taft, his hand-picked successor, giving the election of 1912 to Woodrow Wilson.

5. CALVIN COOLIDGE. Following Warren Harding's sudden death, Coolidge's father, a Justice of the Peace, swore him in as President early on August 3, 1923. In 1924, Coolidge easily won the Republican nomination for his own term and went on to defeat former Ambassador John W. Davis and Senator Robert M. LaFollette (382 electoral votes, 136, and 13, respectively). Coolidge chose not to run for reelection in 1928.

6. HARRY S TRUMAN. John Nance Garner was Franklin Roosevelt's first Vice President, serving 1933–41. He unsuccessfully challenged Roosevelt for the Presidential nomination in 1940. In 1940, Roosevelt chose his Secretary of Agriculture, Henry Agard Wallace, as his Vice Presidential running mate. At the Democratic Convention in 1944, many delegates thought Roosevelt's declining health meant their choice for Vice President would be the next President, and they were unhappy with Wallace in that position. Roosevelt was forced to drop Wallace from the ticket and chose Senator Truman to replace him. Less than three months into his fourth term, Roosevelt died, and Truman was thrust into the Presidency.

Many delegates at the 1948 convention thought Truman was almost unelectable, but when their other choices withdrew their names from consideration, Truman was nominated on the first ballot. He went on to win 49 percent of the popular vote and 303 electoral votes (beating Thomas Dewey [45 percent, 189 electoral votes], Strom Thurmond [2 percent, 39 electoral votes], and former Vice President Wallace [2 percent, 0 electoral votes]).

In 1949, Truman decided not to seek a third term as President, wanting to restore the custom of a two-term Presidency. He announced this decision in March 1952. The 22nd Amendment—limiting the Presidency to two terms, but specifically exempting Truman—was ratified in March 1951.

7. LYNDON BAINES JOHNSON. After running second to John Kennedy for the Democratic Presidential nomination, Kennedy chose him for Vice President. They narrowly defeated the Republican ticket of sitting Vice President Richard Nixon and Henry Cabot Lodge, 49.7 percent to 49.5 percent of the popular vote (303 electoral votes to 219, with 15 being cast for Virginia Senator Harry F. Byrd). Following Kennedy's assassination on November 22, 1963, Johnson became President. He was nominated for his own term by acclamation of the Democratic National Convention in Atlantic City, New Jersey, and went on to defeat Barry Goldwater, 61 percent to 39 percent (486 electoral votes to 52). Johnson chose not to run for another term in 1968, although under the terms of the 22nd Amendment, he was still eligible.

8. RICHARD NIXON. Of the 14 Vice Presidents who later became President, only Nixon ran as a former Vice President. Nixon was Vice President from 1953 to 1961. Inaugurated at the age of 40 years, 11 days, he was the second-youngest man ever to hold the office. Nixon ran for President in the election of 1960, but was defeated by John Kennedy. He lost the 1962 race for the Governorship of California and retired. Then he came back in 1968, narrowly won the Republican Presidential nomination on the first ballot, and defeated sitting Vice President Hubert Humphrey and former Alabama Governor George Wallace in the election (43.4 percent [301 electoral votes] to 42.7 percent [191 electoral votes] to 13.5 percent [46 electoral votes] respectively) to become the only former Vice President to be elected President. In 1972, he handily beat Senator George S. McGovern, 61 percent to 38 percent (520 electoral votes to 17), losing only Massachusetts and the District of Columbia. Facing almost-certain impeachment for his activities surrounding the Watergate scandal, Nixon became the first (and to date, only) President to resign on August 9, 1974. President Ford pardoned him a month later.

9. GEORGE H.W. BUSH. Ronald Reagan went into the 1980 Republican National Convention with the nomination assured. Bush had been his closest challenger during the primaries, but couldn't muster enough support and withdrew his name from consideration before the convention. At the convention, the greatest excitement came from behind-the-scenes negotiations to nominate former President Ford for Vice President, but Ford wasn't very interested in the position and demanded too much for Reagan to accept the deal. Instead, Reagan chose Bush as his running mate. They handily defeated Jimmy Carter's bid for reelection and went on to completely dominate former Vice President Walter Mondale in the election of 1984, winning 525 electoral votes, the most ever. In 1988, Bush easily won the Republican nomination and then beat Massachusetts Governor Michael Dukakis 54 percent to 46 percent (426 electoral votes to 111), becoming the first sitting Vice President to be elected President since Martin Van Buren in 1836. In 1992, Arkansas Governor Bill Clinton blocked Bush's bid for reelection, taking 43 percent of the popular vote to

Bush's 37 percent (independent Ross Perot won 19 percent). The electoral vote count was 370 for Clinton to 168 for Bush (Perot received no electoral votes).

36. The Vice Presidents Who Succeeded to the Presidency but Were Not Elected to Their Own Terms

1. JOHN TYLER. William Henry Harrison won the Whig Presidential nomination again in 1840 (after having lost the election of 1836 to Martin Van Buren). Tyler was nominated for Vice President. Harrison this time defeated Van Buren, but died of pneumonia on April 4, 1841, one month after taking office. Not having been kept apprised of the President's health, Tyler was surprised to be awoken by Fletcher Webster, the Chief Clerk of the Department of State, early on April 5 to be told of Harrison's death. Tyler was at home in Williamsburg, Virginia, and immediately left for Washington, where he was sworn in on April 6. As the first Vice President to succeed, there was much debate over whether Tyler was Acting President or actually President. Tyler determined that he was indeed the President and forced others to come around to his point of view. In 1844, Tyler favored Democrat James Knox Polk over Henry Clay, who received his own party's nomination, so he refused to seek another nomination and retired.

2. MILLARD FILLMORE. Fillmore ran as Whig Zachary Taylor's Vice President, and due to the presence of former President Martin Van Buren running on the Free Soil ticket in the election, they were able to win 47 percent of the popular vote to Democrat Lewis Cass's 43 percent (Van Buren took 10 percent), defeating Cass 163 electoral votes to 127 (Van Buren didn't get any electoral votes). Fillmore visited the ailing President Taylor on July 9, 1850, and realized he was dying. Fillmore was informed of Taylor's death late that evening and sworn in as President at noon on July 10. The Whigs refused to nominate Fillmore for his own term, choosing instead Winfield Scott (who went on to lose to Democrat Franklin Pierce). While on a 13-month excursion to Europe in 1855

and 1856, Fillmore learned that the American Party—also known as the Know-Nothings—had nominated him for President. He returned to the United States in June 1856 to accept the nomination and won 22 percent of the vote (8 electoral votes), coming in third behind winner James Buchanan and John C. Frémont.

3. ANDREW JOHNSON. At the Republican Convention of 1860, Abraham Lincoln was nominated for President on the third ballot, and Hannibal Hamlin was nominated for Vice President. In 1864, Hamlin was surprised to not be renominated, but Lincoln chose Andrew Johnson, a southern Democrat who had remained loyal to the Union, for the second spot on his "National Union" ticket. When the tide turned in the Civil War during the campaign, the Democratic call for an immediate armistice looked like a mistake, and Lincoln won reelection 55 percent to 45 percent over George B. McClellan (212 electoral votes to 21; the 11 states of the Confederacy did not take part in the election). Lincoln was shot on April 14, 1865, and died early the next morning, thrusting Johnson into the Presidency after little more than a month as Vice President.

In 1867, Congress passed—over Johnson's veto—the Tenure of Office Act, forbidding the President to remove anyone from his Cabinet without consent of the Senate. This was a measure passed by the Republicans to attempt to control their non-Republican President. In February 1868, Johnson fired Secretary of War Edwin Stanton, who had been undermining Johnson's policies. On February 24, the House of Representatives voted to impeach Johnson. In May, he was acquitted by one vote, and he served out the remainder of his term. At the Democratic Convention of 1868, the best Johnson could do was 65 votes on the first ballot, less than one-third of the total needed for nomination. Horatio Seymour eventually won the nomination, and Ulysses S. Grant the election.

4. CHESTER ARTHUR. Surprise candidate James Garfield was nominated on the 36th ballot at the Republican Convention in 1880, beating former President Grant, who had been leading (but never by enough) through most of the convention. Chester Arthur was nominated for Vice President in an

attempt to soothe hurt feelings over the Presidential nomination. Garfield and Arthur barely defeated Winfield S. Hancock and William H. English, 48.3 percent to 48.2 percent (a difference of fewer than 10,000 votes out of nearly 9 million). Each ticket won 19 states, but Garfield/Arthur won the Electoral College, 214 to 155. Garfield was shot on July 2, four months into his term, and died of his wounds two months later, on September 19. Arthur learned of the death about an hour later, at 11:30 p.m., and was sworn in about 2:15 the next morning by New York Supreme Court Justice John R. Brady. At that point, there was no Vice President, and because Congress wasn't in session, no President pro tempore of the Senate and no Speaker of the House. Had Arthur died at that point, there would have been no clear successor. To avoid such a catastrophe, Arthur drafted a proclamation calling the Senate into special session and mailed it to the White House. When he arrived in Washington, he was able to destroy the letter and call the Senate into session himself. Arthur was briefly a candidate for his own term in 1884, but his change of heart on several issues virtually guaranteed he would not be nominated. James G. Blaine, who had been Garfield and Arthur's Secretary of State, won the nomination. Democrat Grover Cleveland won the election.

5. GERALD FORD. At the Republican National Convention in 1968, former Vice President Richard Nixon barely won the Presidential nomination on the first ballot. Maryland Governor Spiro Agnew was nominated for Vice President. They won the election 43.4 percent to 42.7 percent (301 electoral votes to 191) over Hubert Humphrey, with George Wallace running a distant third (he won 13.5 percent of the popular vote and 46 electoral votes). In 1972, they were renominated with only token opposition, and then they overwhelmingly beat the Democratic ticket of George S. McGovern and R. Sargent Shriver (61 percent to 38 percent). In October 1973, to avoid prosecution, Vice President Agnew resigned and pleaded no contest to one charge of income-tax evasion. Under the terms of the 25th Amendment (ratified in 1967), Nixon nominated Ford for Vice President in November. The Senate confirmed him in November by a vote of 92 to 3, and the House did so in December, 387 to 35. Ford was sworn in on December 6.

On August 9, 1974, minutes after Nixon's resignation became official, Ford was sworn in as President. A month later, to save the country from what was expected to a drawn-out, messy pretrial and trial should Nixon be indicted, Ford pardoned him. Ford chose Nelson Rockefeller as his Vice President, and he was confirmed in December 1974. In 1975, Rockefeller announced that he would not be a candidate for Vice President the following year. At the 1976 Republican National Convention, Ford was nominated for his own term on the first ballot with 1,187 votes to 1,070 for Ronald Reagan. He chose Senator Robert Dole as his running mate, but they lost to Jimmy Carter and Walter Mondale, 50 percent to 48 percent (297 electoral votes to 240).

At the Republican convention in 1980, nominee Ronald Reagan briefly considered Ford for his Vice Presidential running mate, but Ford wasn't interested and made such absurd demands that negotiations broke down, and Reagan chose George H.W. Bush.

37. The Vice Presidents Who Had Never Held Elective Office before Being Elected Vice President

1. CHESTER A. ARTHUR (1881). After graduating from New York's Union College, he was a school principal and then a lawyer. During the Civil War, he was the Quartermaster General of New York and then the Inspector General with the rank of a Brigadier General. After the war, President Grant appointed him Collector of Customs for the Port of New York, which post he held from 1871 to 1878. Arthur was Vice President for only six months before James Garfield died, and he succeeded to the Presidency.

2. CHARLES G. DAWES (1925–29). Dawes graduated from Marietta College and later the Cincinnati Law School. He was a banker and a lawyer. Following his support of William McKinley in the election of 1896, he was appointed Comptroller of the Currency (1898–1901). Dawes served in the US Army during World War I, where he rose to the rank of Brigadier General. He resigned from the Army in 1919, and was appointed the first Director of the US Bureau of the Budget (1921–23). Following that, he was appointed to the Allied Reparations Committee (1923–25) and then was elected Vice President when Calvin Coolidge ran for his own term as President. Following his one term in office, Dawes was appointed Ambassador to the United Kingdom, where he served from 1929 to 1932.

3. HENRY A. WALLACE (1941–45). Wallace was a newspaper editor, a graduate of Iowa State College at Ames, and an agricultural researcher. He co-founded Hi-Bred Corn, which later became the Pioneer Hi-Bred company, and in 1933, President Franklin Roosevelt appointed him the 11th Secretary of Agriculture (Wallace's father, Henry C., had been the seventh Secretary, from 1921 to 1924). Wallace resigned from the Cabinet

in 1940, when he became the Democratic nominee for Vice President (Roosevelt and his first Vice President, John Nance Garner, had had a falling out). Wallace served one term as Vice President and then was replaced on the ticket in 1944 by Harry Truman. Following the election of 1944 and Roosevelt's fourth inauguration, he appointed Wallace the 10th Secretary of Commerce (though Truman fired him a year and a half later). After leaving government, Wallace edited *The New Republic* magazine for two years.

38. The Vice Presidents
Who Won Nobel Prizes

1. THEODORE ROOSEVELT (1901). Roosevelt won the 1906 Nobel Peace Prize for his success in mediating the Treaty of Portsmouth as President. The treaty ended the Russo-Japanese War of 1904–05, which had been fought over control of Manchuria and Korea. Roosevelt was the first American to win the six-year-old prize. He used the prize money ($36,735) to create a trust fund to promote international peace. After the United States entered World War I, he diverted the now-$45,000 trust to aid war victims. His medal is on display in the Roosevelt Room of the White House.

2. CHARLES DAWES (1925–29). Dawes was born in 1865 in Ohio, a son of Civil War General Rufus Dawes. He was the US Comptroller of the Currency from 1898 to 1901, collecting millions of dollars from banks that had failed during the Panic of 1893, and changing banking practices to try to prevent a similar event in the future. He left the Treasury Department to run for a seat in the Senate, but lost. During World War I, Dawes served as an Engineering Officer in France, and in October 1918, was promoted to Brigadier General. As a General, he was Chairman of the General Purchasing Board for the American Expeditionary Forces, a member of the Military Board of Allied Supply, and after the war, a member of the Liquidation Commission of the US War Department. He resigned from the Army in 1919. Dawes was appointed the first Director of the Bureau of the Budget, in 1921, and to the Allied Reparations Commission in 1923. In that post, he created the Dawes Plan, which was a program designed to enable Germany to restore and stabilize its economy, putting its reparations payments on an installment plan. Ultimately, the Dawes Plan was deemed unworkable and replaced in 1929, but the Plan earned Dawes a share of the Nobel Peace Prize in 1925.

3. AL GORE (1993–2001). Gore was a Representative (1977–85), Senator (1985–93), and the 45th Vice President (1993–2001). He was the Democratic nominee for President in 2000, and lost a controversial election to George W. Bush. A lifelong environmentalist, he became more active and used his high profile in environmental causes after leaving government service. In 2004 he co-launched Generation Investment Management, an investment firm that blends traditional equity research with a focus on sustainability, including social and environmental responsibility and corporate governance. He also founded The Alliance for Climate Protection with proceeds from his book and film *An Inconvenient Truth*. He shared the 2007 Nobel Peace Prize with the Intergovernmental Panel on Climate Change "for their efforts to build up and disseminate greater knowledge about man-made climate change, and to lay the foundations for the measures that are needed to counteract such change."

THE VICE PRESIDENTS: ON THE JOB

39. The Five Oldest Vice Presidents

Considered by age at inauguration, the list runs as follows:

1. ALBEN W. BARKLEY (1949–53) was 71 years, 57 days old when he was inaugurated as Harry Truman's Vice President on January 20, 1949. He was more than a year older, at inauguration, than the oldest President (Ronald Reagan, who was a month shy of his 70th birthday at his inauguration) and seven years older than his President.

2. CHARLES CURTIS (1929–33) was 69 years, 38 days old when he and President Herbert Hoover were inaugurated on March 4, 1929. He was 14 years older than Hoover, who outlived him by 28 years. Curtis was also the first national officeholder who was not of completely European descent. Much of his heritage was Native American, specifically Kaw.

3. ELBRIDGE GERRY (1813–14), the fifth Vice President, was 68 years, 230 days old when he was inaugurated as James Madison's second Vice President. His predecessor, George Clinton, was the first Vice President to die in office. Gerry was the second, dying on November 23, 1814, after serving only one year, 264 days.

4. WILLIAM R.D. KING (1853) was 66 years, 331 days old when he took office with Franklin Pierce on March 4, 1853. King served the shortest term of all the Vice Presidents who did not succeed to the Presidency. He died on April 18, 1853, 45 days after taking office (having never made it to the national capital during his Vice Presidency).

5. NELSON A. ROCKEFELLER (1974–77) was 66 years, 164 days old when he became the second Vice President to take office under the terms of the 25th Amendment. His predecessor and President, Gerald Ford, was the first. Rockefeller was sworn into the Vice Presidency on December 19, 1974, 132 days after Ford became President. To knock him off the list, the Vice President elected in 2016 will have to have been born before August 9, 1951.

Current Vice President JOE BIDEN just misses this list. He was 66 years, 61 days old when he was inaugurated on January 20, 2009.

However, considering age at the time the Vice President left office, Barkley and Curtis maintain their places, but Gerry drops to fifth (he was 70 years, 192 days old when he died in office). Fourth Vice President George Clinton (1805–12) moves into third place; he was only 65 years, 144 days old when he was inaugurated, putting him seventh on the list, but he served a little more than seven years before dying in office on April 20, 1812, at the age of 72 years, 268 days. Also, Franklin Roosevelt's first Vice President, John Nance Garner (the longest-lived Vice President), served two full terms, leaving office on January 20, 1941, at the age of 72 years, 59 days.

Joe Biden is still in office, but his 73rd birthday was November 20, 2015. He will be the second oldest to retire from the office on January 20, 2017.

40. The Five Youngest Vice Presidents

Like the President he serves under, the Vice President must be at least 35 years old.

1. JOHN C. BRECKINRIDGE (1857–61) was 36 years, 318 days old when he was inaugurated with President James Buchanan. Breckinridge's predecessor, William R. King, is #4 on the list of oldest Vice Presidents. To beat Breckinridge's record as the youngest Vice President in the election of 2016, the newly elected Vice President will have to have been born after March 8, 1980 (but Constitutionally, will be required to have been born before January 20, 1982).

2. RICHARD M. NIXON (1953–61) was 40 years, 11 days old when he was inaugurated with President Dwight Eisenhower (who was the second-oldest President when he left office). Nixon was the only Vice President to later become President without moving directly from the former office to the latter.

3. JAMES DANFORTH QUAYLE (1989–93) was 41 years, 350 days old when he was inaugurated with President George H.W. Bush (who was also his Vice Presidential predecessor). Quayle was the first Vice President to be born after the end of World War II.

4. THEODORE ROOSEVELT (1901) was 42 years, 128 days old when he was inaugurated as William McKinley's second Vice President (his predecessor, Garret A. Hobart, had died in office). Six months later, McKinley was assassinated, and Roosevelt became the youngest President ever.

5. DANIEL D. TOMPKINS (1817–25) was 42 years, 256 days old when he and President James Monroe were inaugurated. Tompkins, the sixth Vice

President, was the youngest to date. His two immediate predecessors, George Clinton and Elbridge Gerry, were among the oldest, and both had died in office.

JOHN C. CALHOUN (1825–32) just misses this list. He was 42 years, 351 days old when he was inaugurated.

In order to join this list (and knock Tompkins off), the Vice President who wins the election of 2016 will have to have been born after May 9, 1974.

41. The Vice Presidents Who Shared Birthdays/Deathdays with Presidents

Five days saw the birth of at least one Vice President and one President, and five different days the death of at least one of each. Truly red-letter days include August 27, on which three Vice Presidents (one of whom later became President) were born, and July 4, on which three Presidents and one other Vice President died.

Birthdays:

JANUARY 30: President Franklin Roosevelt (1933–45) was born in 1882. Vice President Richard "Dick" Cheney (2001–09) was born in 1941.

FEBRUARY 6: Vice President Aaron Burr (1801–05) was born in 1756. President Ronald Reagan (1981–89) was born in 1911.

MARCH 18: Vice President John Calhoun (1825–33) was born in 1782. President Grover Cleveland (1885–89, 1893–97) was born in 1837.

AUGUST 27: Vice President Hannibal Hamlin (1861–65) was born in 1809. Vice President Charles Dawes (1925–29) was born in 1865. And President (and former Vice President) Lyndon Johnson (1963–69) was born in 1908.

NOVEMBER 24: President Zachary Taylor (1849–50) was born in 1784. Vice President Alben Barkley (1949–53) was born in 1877.

Deathdays:

JUNE 1: President James Buchanan (1857–61) died in 1868. Vice President Thomas Marshall (1913–21) died in 1925.

JULY 4: Presidents (and former Vice Presidents) John Adams (1797–1801) and Thomas Jefferson (1801–09) both died in 1826. President James Monroe (1817–25) died in 1831. Vice President Hannibal Hamlin (1861–65) died in 1891.

SEPTEMBER 14: Vice President Aaron Burr (1801–05) died in 1836. President William McKinley (1897–1901) died in 1901.

NOVEMBER 18: President (and former Vice President) Chester Arthur (1881–85) died in 1886. Vice President Henry Wallace (1941–45) died in 1965.

NOVEMBER 22: Vice President Henry Wilson (1873–75) died in 1875. President John Kennedy (1961–63) died in 1963. Both these men died in office.

42. The Five Vice Presidents Who Were the Greatest Number of Years Older Than Their Predecessors

1. GEORGE CLINTON was 16 years, 195 days older than Aaron Burr. Clinton was born July 26, 1739, and served 1805–12 (he died in office). Burr was born February 6, 1756, and served 1801–05.

2. WILLIAM KING was 13 years, 275 days older than Millard Fillmore. King was born April 7, 1786, and served in March and April 1853, dying in office. Fillmore was born January 7, 1800, and served in 1849 and 1850, succeeding to the Presidency.

3. HANNIBAL HAMLIN was 11 years, 142 days older than John Breckinridge. Hamlin was born August 27, 1809, and served 1861–65. Breckinridge was born January 16, 1821, and served 1857–61.

4. HENRY WILSON was 11 years, 35 days older than Schuyler Colfax. Wilson was born February 16, 1812, and served 1873–75 (he died in office). Colfax was born March 23, 1823, and served 1869–73.

5. THOMAS HENDRICKS was 11 years, 28 days older than Chester Arthur. Hendricks was born September 7, 1819, and served in 1885 (he died in office). Arthur was born October 5, 1830, and served in 1881 (before succeeding to the Presidency).

43. The Five Vice Presidents Who Were the Greatest Number of Years Younger Than Their Predecessors

1. RICHARD M. NIXON was 35 years, 46 days younger than Alben W. Barkley. Nixon was born January 9, 1913, and served 1953–61. Barkley was born November 24, 1877, and served 1949–53.

2. JOHN C. BRECKINRIDGE was 34 years, 284 days younger than William King. Breckinridge was born January 16, 1821, and served 1857–61. King was born April 7, 1786, and served in March and April 1853, dying in office.

3. DANIEL TOMPKINS was 29 years, 339 days younger than Elbridge Gerry. Tompkins was born June 21, 1774, and served 1817–25. Gerry was born July 17, 1744, and served 1813–14, dying in office.

4. DAN QUAYLE was 22 years, 237 days younger than George H.W. Bush (who was both his predecessor as Vice President and the President under whom he served). Quayle was born February 4, 1947, and served 1989–93. Bush was born June 12, 1924, and served 1981–89.

5. HENRY WALLACE was 19 years, 339 days younger than John Garner. Wallace was born October 7, 1888, and served as Franklin Roosevelt's second Vice President, from 1941 to 1945. Garner was born November 22, 1868, and was Roosevelt's first Vice President, from 1933 to 1941.

44. The Five Vice Presidents Who Were the Greatest Number of Years Older Than Their Presidents

The Vice President's chief Constitutional duty is to be available in case he has to step in to replace the President, and since all the Presidents who've left office mid-term (but one) died in office, one might assume that having a Vice President younger than his President would be *de rigueur*. On the other hand, perhaps an older Vice Presidential candidate can balance the relative youth of a young-ish Presidential candidate. In any case, 23 of the 47 Vice Presidents were older than their Presidents.

1. JOE BIDEN (2009–) is 18 years, 257 days older than Barack Obama. Forty-seven-year-old Obama is the fifth-youngest President to take office, while 66-year-old Biden is the sixth-oldest Vice President to take office.

2. WILLIAM KING (1853) was 18 years, 230 days older than Franklin Pierce. King had served in the Senate for nearly 30 years and supported Pierce's opponent for the nomination, James Buchanan. King was chosen for the Vice Presidential slot to maintain party unity. King died in April 1853, two weeks after his 67th birthday, less than two months after Inauguration Day.

3. THOMAS A. HENDRICKS (1885) was 17 years, 192 days older than Grover Cleveland. Hendricks died less than nine months into his term, during which he celebrated his 66th birthday. Cleveland at the time was the second-youngest President ever (after Ulysses Grant); now he's sixth on the list of youngest Presidents.

4. CHARLES CURTIS was (1929–33) was 14 years, 197 days than Herbert Hoover. The second oldest of all the Vice Presidents (he was 69 when he was inaugurated), he was also a retired Vice President for three years.

5.JOHN NANCE GARNER (1933–41) was 13 years, 69 days older than Franklin Delano Roosevelt. The longest lived of the Vice Presidents, he retired at the age of 72 years, 59 days, the fifth oldest Vice President to leave office. He was dropped from the ticket, because he differed with Roosevelt's decision to run for a third term: Garner wanted to be President (he would have been the oldest ever, but he lived to nearly 99 years of age, so that might not have been a problem).

Two other Vice Presidents were more than 10 years older than their Presidents:

GEORGE CLINTON (1805–12) served under Thomas Jefferson and James Madison, and he was older than both of them. He was 11 years, 233 days older than James Madison and died in office (Madison's second Vice President, Elbridge Gerry, also died in office).

HENRY WILSON (1873–75) was 10 years, 70 days older than Ulysses Grant. Wilson was added to the ticket for Grant's second term, after Schuyler Colfax was caught in the Crédit Mobilier scandal and dropped from the ticket. Grant was the youngest to be elected President at the time, though he's now #4 on that list.

45. The Vice Presidents Who Died in Office

Eight of the 43 Presidents died in office (William Henry Harrison in 1841, Zachary Taylor in 1850, Abraham Lincoln in 1865, James Garfield in 1881, William McKinley in 1901, Warren Harding in 1923, Franklin Roosevelt in 1945, and John Kennedy in 1963). And though we've had more Vice Presidents (47), only seven of them have died in office:

1. GEORGE CLINTON (1805–12). Fourth Vice President George Clinton was Thomas Jefferson's second Vice President (Jefferson chose Clinton to replace Aaron Burr for his second term). Clinton was the first of two Vice Presidents to serve two different Presidents, as he ran with James Madison for Madison's first term. Clinton died in office, of a heart attack, on April 20, 1812, aged 72 years, 268 days. Born in 1739, he had been the oldest Vice President to take office.

2. ELBRIDGE GERRY (1813–14). Following Clinton's death, James Madison chose Gerry as his running mate, and they won the election of 1812. Gerry was the last signer of the Declaration of Independence to serve as Vice President, taking office on March 4, 1813, at the age of 68. On November 23, 1814, he collapsed on his way to the Senate and died in the Capitol, the first Vice President to serve less than one full term.

3. WILLIAM R.D. KING (1853). King had resigned his seat in the Senate in December 1852 due to his failing health. He traveled to Cuba in hopes of finding a cure for his tuberculosis and took the oath of office there— by special Congressional dispensation—on March 24, 1853. He returned to his plantation in mid-April and died on the 18th. His 45 days as Vice President (his term started on March 4, even though he took the oath three weeks later) was the shortest term of any Vice President (other than John

Tyler and Andrew Johnson, who succeeded to the Presidency upon the deaths of their Presidents). He's also the only Vice President to never make it to the national capital while he was Vice President.

4. HENRY WILSON (1873–75). Aged 61 when he took office as Ulysses Grant's second Vice President on March 4, 1873 (Grant dropped Schuyler Colfax from the ticket for his second term), Wilson suffered a stroke that May, but refused his doctor's orders to get enough rest and suffered partial paralysis the rest of his life. On November 10, 1875, he suffered a sudden total paralysis in the Senate. He recovered a bit, but died in his office on November 22, 1875.

5. THOMAS A. HENDRICKS (1885). He was Grover Cleveland's first Vice President, but served only 266 days. He was inaugurated on March 4, 1885, and was at home in Indianapolis, Indiana, when he died in his sleep on November 25 of that year, aged 66 years, 79 days.

6. GARRET A. HOBART (1897–99). He died younger than any other Vice President who died in office. Hobart took office on March 4, 1897, with William McKinley, and then died of heart failure on November 21, 1899, aged 51 years, 171 days. His death cleared the way for Theodore Roosevelt to be McKinley's second Vice President and then to succeed to the Presidency following McKinley's assassination.

7. JAMES S. SHERMAN (1909–12). He was William Howard Taft's Vice President from their inauguration on March 4, 1909. Sherman's health steadily declined—although he hid it well—from a bout of gallstones and kidney trouble in 1908. Sherman succumbed on October 30, 1912, a week before the election that saw Taft lose his bid for reelection. It wasn't Sherman's death that cost Taft the election so much as the presence of his predecessor, Theodore Roosevelt, who split the Republican vote, giving Democrat Woodrow Wilson the election.

46. The Vice Presidents Who Served Two Full Terms

Of the 46 people to have completed their terms as Vice President, only six have served two complete, four-year terms as one eight-year block each: DANIEL D. TOMPKINS (1817–25), THOMAS R. MARSHALL (1913–21), RICHARD M. NIXON (1953-61), GEORGE H.W. BUSH (1981–89), ALBERT GORE, JR. (1993–2001), and RICHARD B. CHENEY (2001–09).

First Vice President JOHN ADAMS is not on this list, because his first term wasn't four years long. The election of the first President (and Vice President) came in early 1789, soon after the Constitution was ratified. By the time Adams was notified of his election and reported to New York City (then the capital), it was well into April. In fact, Adams arrived before President-elect George Washington and was inaugurated as Vice President on April 21, 1789 (Washington, arriving later, was inaugurated on April 30, 1789). They were reelected in 1792, and served out the first two terms, but because their first was less than four years long (April 21, 1789–March 4, 1793), he doesn't belong on the list.

JOHN C. CALHOUN was the first Vice President to resign from office. He was the second of two Vice Presidents to serve two different Presidents. His first term was under John Quincy Adams, and his second was Andrew Jackson's first term. He and Jackson split during the term, and Jackson chose Martin Van Buren as his Vice Presidential running mate for his second term. Calhoun was elected to the Senate and resigned the Vice Presidency on December 28, 1832, three months before the end of his second term, in order to take his seat in the Senate.

JOHN NANCE GARNER was Franklin Delano Roosevelt's first Vice President. Together, they won the elections of 1932 and 1936. They split during the second term over Roosevelt's decision to run for an unprecedented third term (Garner wanted to run for President), and Roosevelt dropped him from the ticket for the third election. The 20th Amendment, changing inauguration day from March 4 to January 20, was ratified on January 23, 1933. This change shortened that term. Thus, Garner served as Vice President from March 4, 1933, to January 20, 1941.

47. The Five Vice Presidents Who Served the Shortest Terms

1. JOHN TYLER was Vice President for a scant 31 days. He and President William Henry Harrison were inaugurated on a very rainy March 4, 1841, during which Harrison spoke (without a hat or coat) outdoors for almost two hours. He developed pneumonia and died on April 4, 1841. Harrison was the first President to die in office, and at the time, there was some question as to whether the Vice President would be Acting President for the remainder of the term or would succeed to the office as President. Tyler, by force of will, proved it was the latter, and he was the 10th President for nearly four years.

2. ANDREW JOHNSON was Abraham Lincoln's choice as a running mate in his reelection campaign of 1864. Looking back on that election from a century and a half in the future, it's hard to believe Lincoln was in a close race, but there were times during the campaign when his defeat looked probable. He dropped Hannibal Hamlin from the Republican ticket in order to make room for a loyal Southerner—and a Democrat, to boot—hoping that would be enough to ensure his reelection. Lincoln also dropped the brand new "Republican" label, calling his ticket the "National Union" party. Good news from the Civil War late in the campaign ensured Lincoln's reelection, and just over a month after his second inauguration, the Confederacy surrendered. Days later, John Wilkes Booth shot Lincoln to death, and Andrew Johnson was thrust into the Presidency after only 42 days as Vice President.

3. WILLIAM RUFUS DEVANE KING served the shortest term of all Vice Presidents who did not succeed to the Presidency. He was also the only one to take the oath of office on foreign soil. King had been a member of the Senate for 28 years when he was elected Vice President with Franklin

Pierce in 1852. Suffering from tuberculosis, he hoped a change of climate would do him good and went to Cuba after the election. It didn't help, and he stayed in Cuba. In mid-March 1853, having missed inauguration day, Congress authorized him to take the oath of office in Cuba. He returned home to Alabama on April 16, and died on April 18, 1853. He was Vice President for 45 days and the only national officeholder to never make it to the capital during his term.

4. HARRY S TRUMAN was Franklin Roosevelt's third Vice President, put on the ticket because the leaders of the Democratic Party feared Roosevelt wouldn't survive a fourth term in the White House, and they did not want to see Vice President Wallace become President. Roosevelt bowed to their pressure to drop Wallace and chose the Senator from Missouri. Roosevelt and Truman were inaugurated (for the fourth and first times, respectively) on January 20, 1945. Roosevelt did indeed die, on April 12, and Harry Truman became President after only 82 days as Vice President.

5. THEODORE ROOSEVELT was pushed onto William McKinley's ticket in the election of 1900 by Boss Platt, who did not want the young reformer stirring up trouble for him as Governor of New York. McKinley's first Vice President, Garret Hobart, had died in office. Roosevelt reluctantly accepted the nomination, and on March 4, 1901, became the second-youngest Vice President (Richard Nixon and Dan Quayle later won the office at younger ages than Roosevelt). On September 6, while visiting the Pan American Exhibition in Buffalo, New York, McKinley was shot at point-blank range by Leon Czolgosz. Roosevelt was with his family on the other side of the state and rushed to the President's side. He was reassured that McKinley was alive and looked to stay that way, and returned to his family. On September 14, however, McKinley died of gangrene at the sites of his bullet wounds, making Roosevelt the youngest President ever after only 194 days as Vice President.

Three other Vice Presidents served terms of less than one year:

CHESTER A. ARTHUR was elected Vice President in 1880. President James Garfield was shot on July 2, 1881, and died on September 19, making Arthur the 21st President after 199 days as Vice President.

GERALD R. FORD was the first Vice President to be appointed under the terms of the 25th Amendment. Following Spiro Agnew's resignation, President Richard Nixon tapped the House Minority Leader to be his second Vice President. Ford was confirmed by Congress and took the oath of office on December 6, 1973. In August 1974, Nixon stunned the world by announcing his resignation, and Ford was sworn into that office on August 9, 1974, after a Vice Presidency of 246 days.

THOMAS A. HENDRICKS was Grover Cleveland's first Vice President; they were elected in 1884. He suffered a stroke and became the fifth Vice President to die in office on November 25, 1885, after serving 266 days.

48. The Times There Was No Vice President

Since the beginning of Presidents and Vice Presidents, the Presidency has been occupied nearly continuously. The longest periods of time without a President in the office were the first, before George Washington was inaugurated (he first took the oath of office nine days after first Vice President John Adams), and then following President William Henry Harrison's death in office, when it took Vice President John Tyler nearly two days to be notified and make his way to Washington, DC, to be inaugurated.

Gaps in the Vice Presidency, however, have been far more common and of far greater duration. Indeed, before the adoption of the 25th Amendment in 1967, there was no Constitutional mechanism to fill a vacancy in the Vice Presidency. Admittedly, before 1973, there was never any need. Now it can be done, through Presidential appointment and the concurrence of Congress. Before 1967, vacancies in the office were left unfilled until the next election (the Senate chose a President pro tempore to handle the Vice President's only other Constitutional duty).

From 1789 to 2015, we've had 44 Presidents and 47 Vice Presidents. In that time, there have been 18 vacancies in the Vice Presidency. The first came when fourth Vice President George Clinton died in office, more than three years into his second term, on April 20, 1812. The following vacancy lasted 318 days, until Elbridge Gerry was inaugurated. Gerry's death, on November 23, 1814, left the office vacant for two years, 101 days.

The Vice Presidency has been vacant due to seven Vice Presidential deaths in office, eight Presidential deaths in office (resulting in the Vice Presidents succeeding to the office), two Vice Presidential resignations from office (John Calhoun, at the end of 1832, to take his seat in the Senate, and Spiro Agnew, in 1973, as part of a plea deal), and one Presidential resignation from office. The last two vacancies were the first to be filled by appointing a new Vice President, rather than waiting for a new election, so the era of multi-year vacancies in the office is probably over. Nevertheless, in the two and a quarter centuries we've operated under our current system of government, the Vice Presidency has been vacant for 37 years, 295 days, or about 17 percent of the time.

The longest times the country was without a Vice President were:

1. Three years, 335 days. From April 4, 1841, to March 4, 1845 (from the death of President William Henry Harrison and the succession of Vice President John Tyler, until the election of James Polk and George M. Dallas).

2. Three years, 323 days. From April 15, 1865, to March 4, 1869 (from the death of President Abraham Lincoln and the succession of Vice President Andrew Johnson, until the election of Ulysses Grant and Schuyler Colfax).

3. Three years, 320 days. From April 18, 1853, to March 4, 1857 (from the death of Vice President William Rufus DeVane King, until the election of James Buchanan and John C. Breckinridge).

4. Three years, 283 days. From April 12, 1945, to January 20, 1949 (from the death of President Franklin Delano Roosevelt and the succession of Vice President Harry S Truman, until Truman's election as President with Alben W. Barkley).

5. Three years, 171 days. From September 14, 1901, to March 4, 1905 (from the death of President William McKinley and the succession of Vice President Theodore Roosevelt, until Roosevelt's election as President with Charles W. Fairbanks).

From September 19, 1881, to March 4, 1889, seven and a half years, there was a Vice President for only 266 days. After James Garfield's death in

1881, Chester Arthur assumed the Presidency. Following his term, Grover Cleveland and Thomas A. Hendricks were elected President and Vice President. Hendricks died on November 25, 1885, less than nine months after taking office, and the Vice Presidency was again vacant until Benjamin Harrison and Levi Morton took office.

From July 9, 1850, to March 4, 1857, six and two-thirds years, there was a Vice President for only 45 days. After Zachary Taylor's death in 1850, Millard Fillmore assumed the Presidency. Following his term, Franklin Pierce and William King were elected President and Vice President. King died 45 days after inauguration day, again leaving the Vice Presidency vacant until James Buchanan and John C. Breckinridge took office.

The shortest Vice Presidential vacancies were:

1. 57 days. From October 10 to December 6, 1973 (from the resignation of Vice President Spiro T. Agnew, until Gerald R. Ford was sworn to replace him).

2. 67 days. From December 28, 1832, to March 4, 1833 (from the resignation of Vice President John C. Calhoun, until the inauguration of Vice President Martin Van Buren).

3. 125 days. From October 30, 1912, to March 4, 1913 (from the death of Vice President James S. Sherman, until the inauguration of Woodrow Wilson and Thomas R. Marshall).

4. 132 days. From August 9 to December 19, 1974 (from the resignation of President Richard Nixon and the succession of Vice President Gerald Ford, until Nelson Rockefeller was sworn into the Vice Presidency).

5. 318 days. From April 20, 1812, to March 4, 1813 (from the death of Vice President George Clinton, until the inauguration of Vice President Elbridge Gerry).

49. The Longest Terms with No Vice Presidential Vacancies

Having been without a Vice President for 17 percent of the time (37 years, 295 days), it almost seems as if vacancies in the Vice Presidency are common. And the first came a scant 23 years after the inauguration of the first Vice President (when fourth Vice President George Clinton died in office, on April 20, 1812). The first Presidential death in office wasn't until 1841.

1. 41 years+. From December 19, 1974, to now. Starting with Nelson Rockefeller's inauguration (as the third Vice President during the 1973–77 Presidential term), no Vice President has left office before the end of the term to which he was elected. Those six Vice Presidents also represent the greatest number of successive Vice Presidents to complete their terms in a row in history: Rockefeller, Walter Mondale, George H.W. Bush, Dan Quayle, Al Gore, and Dick Cheney. Plus, at the time of this writing, Joe Biden, too, is going strong.

2. 27 years, 21 days. From April 21, 1789, to April 20, 1812. From the inauguration of the first Vice President, John Adams, until fourth Vice President George Clinton became the first to die in office.

3. 20 years, 39 days. From March 4, 1925, to April 12, 1945. From the inauguration of Charles Dawes through his four successors. This was also the first (and other than now, only) time in history when as many as four Vice Presidents served out complete terms. After Dawes came Charles Curtis, John Nance Garner, and Henry A. Wallace. Then Harry S Truman, President Franklin Roosevelt's third Vice President, served a scant 82 days before Roosevelt's death in office.

4. 15 years, 299 days. From March 4, 1817, to December 28, 1832. Following two Vice Presidential deaths in office, the country elected 42-year-old Daniel D. Tompkins—the youngest ever at the time—to the office, and he survived a full eight years. His successor, John C. Calhoun, also survived eight years, but he resigned more than two months before his term ended in order to take the seat he'd just been elected to in the Senate.

5. 14 years, 306 days. From January 20, 1949, to November 22, 1963. After Harry Truman succeeded to the Presidency, he served his first term without a Vice President and then was elected to his own term with Vice President Alben Barkley. Barkley was succeeded by Richard Nixon, the second-youngest Vice President ever. Nixon lost the Presidential election of 1960 to John Kennedy, the youngest President ever elected, but when Kennedy was assassinated, Vice President Lyndon Baines Johnson moved up, again leaving the Vice Presidency vacant.

50. The Vice Presidents Who Served under Two Presidents

Now we elect them as a pair: President and Vice President. They run as a ticket, get elected as a ticket, and sometimes get defeated as a ticket. But there's nothing requiring them to be paired only with one another. Due to death, resignation, or other political considerations, nine Presidents had more than one Vice President. But looking the other way, it's much more rare for Vice Presidents to have more than one President. Indeed, only two of them have.

GEORGE CLINTON, who was Vice President from 1805 to 1812, was the fourth Vice President. He got the job in the election of 1804, which was Thomas Jefferson's second as President. Before 1804, the Vice President was the candidate who won the second-greatest number of electoral votes in the election. But in the election of 1800, the Democrat-Republican Congressmen nominated the Vice President, Thomas Jefferson, for the Presidency, and the ticket of Thomas Jefferson and Aaron Burr beat sitting President John Adams running with Charles Cotesworth Pinckney. Jefferson/Burr won handily. Unfortunately, Jefferson and Burr each received 73 electoral votes. And even though the ticket was Jefferson for President and Burr for Vice President, the tie threw the election to the House of Representatives, and Burr refused to concede. Eventually, a majority of the House chose Jefferson, but these events soured Jefferson and Burr's relationship. In 1804, to prevent such a problem from cropping up again, the 12th Amendment was adopted, which provided for the electors to vote separately for President and Vice President. Jefferson and Clinton were the first ticket elected under the new system. In 1808, Jefferson bowed to George Washington's precedent and announced his retirement, and the Democrat-Republican Congressmen nominated

James Monroe for the Presidency, renominating Clinton for the Vice Presidency. On April 20, 1812, Clinton became the first Vice President to die in office.

JOHN C. CALHOUN, who was Vice President from 1825 to 1832, was the seventh Vice President. In the disputed four-way election of 1824, Calhoun may have taken the easiest way to office, opting out of a run for the Presidency and instead running for Vice President. While the four major Presidential candidates divided the Electoral College and forced the election again to the House of Representatives (which ultimately chose John Quincy Adams, even though Andrew Jackson had more electoral votes), Calhoun won the Vice Presidency in a landslide, winning 182 of the 260 electoral votes (beating a field of Henry Clay, Andrew Jackson, Nathaniel Macon, Nathan Sanford, and Martin Van Buren). During their term, Adams and Calhoun's differing opinions became obvious, and in the election of 1828, Calhoun, the sitting Vice President, ran with Presidential challenger Andrew Jackson. Jackson and Calhoun won easily, and Calhoun began serving under his second President. During their term, however, their differences, too, became apparent, and when Jackson ran for reelection in 1832, he chose Martin Van Buren as his running mate. Late in 1832, the South Carolina legislature elected Calhoun to the US Senate, and he resigned the Vice Presidency on December 28, 1832, to take his seat in that body. Calhoun was the only Vice President to resign until Spiro Agnew resigned in a plea deal to avoid prosecution for corruption, in 1973.

51. Vice Presidential Tie-Breakers

One task that is uniquely the Vice President's is presiding over the Senate. And in carrying out that duty, one of the few jobs that is not delegated or purely ceremonial is breaking tied votes. Indeed, that task is specifically spelled out in the Constitution. Article I, Section 3 says: "The Vice President of the United States shall be President of the Senate, but shall have no Vote, unless they be equally divided." And in the early days of the Republic, it was not merely an honorary job. John Adams, as the first President of the Senate, cast 29 tie-breaking votes (out of 317 recorded votes), more than any of his successors. He was a very active President of the Senate, writing legislation, participating in debates, lobbying for votes, and frequently lecturing the Senate on procedural and policy matters. Late in his term, a resolution was bruited about that would limit his participation to procedural and policy matters, so Adams voluntarily toned down his participation.

His successor, Thomas Jefferson, was less active in the day-to-day activity of the Senate. He began the enduring Vice Presidential tradition of only attending Senate sessions on special occasions. Nevertheless, he left a substantial mark on the body: during his term as President of the Senate, Jefferson assembled a volume parliamentary procedure for the Senate's use. On February 27, 1801 (days before he left the Vice Presidency to become the third President), his printer delivered Jefferson's *Manual of Parliamentary Practice for the Use of the Senate of the United States.*

Since that time, presiding over the Senate seems to have diminished in the public's mind when considering the role of the Vice President. Nowadays, those Senate Presidents are most visible during the Presidents' State of the Union addresses (when they share the elevated seat behind the speaking President with the Speaker of the House). Nevertheless, Vice Presidents do still occasionally cast tie-breaking votes, and in the 226 years since John Adams took office, 35 Vice Presidents have cast a total of 244 tie-breaking votes.

The Vice Presidents Who Cast the Most Tie-Breaking Votes in the Senate:

1. JOHN ADAMS (1789–97). The first Vice President was the most active President of the Senate. In just under eight years on the job, he cast 29 tie-breaking votes (an average of 3.7 such votes per year).

2. JOHN C. CALHOUN (1825–32). In just under eight years on the job (he resigned as President of the Senate two months before his term of office ended, in order to take his seat as a member of the Senate), he cast 28 tie-breaking votes.

3. GEORGE M. DALLAS (1845–49). In one four-year term, Dallas cast 19 tie-breaking votes (an average of 4.75 per year).

4 (tie). RICHARD M. JOHNSON (1837–41). Johnson served four years and cast 17 tie-breaking votes (4.25 per year).

4 (tie). SCHUYLER COLFAX (1869–73). Colfax, too, served four years and cast 17 tie-breaking votes.

But the number of recorded, or roll-call, votes (and thus, opportunities for there to be a tie vote that a Vice President must break) is not constant. The number of recorded votes in the Senate varies from a low of 52 in the second Congress (1790–91) to a high of 986 in the 47th Congress (1881–82). Starting in 1947, we have data for the number of recorded votes by year (as opposed to per two-year Congress): in this era, the fewest was 88 in 1955, and the most was 700 in 1976.

Considering tie-breaking votes as a percentage of total votes, John Adams retains his spot as the #1 tie-breaker with an astounding 9.15 percent of recorded votes being ties (Adams cast 29 votes out of 317 total recorded votes). Numbers 2 and 3 reverse positions: George Dallas cast 19 tie-breaking votes out of 727 total votes (2.61 percent), while John Calhoun cast 28 tie-breakers out of 1,171 votes (2.39 percent), but Dallas served four years, while Calhoun served eight. Richard Johnson maintains fourth place; his 17 votes out of 744 is 2.28 percent. But fifth and sixth place are very close: two Vice Presidents who served incomplete terms. Elbridge Gerry, who served 20 months, cast six tie-breaking votes out of approximately 263 votes (about 2.28 percent); George Clinton, who served seven years, cast 12 tie-breaking votes out of 550 chances (about 2.18 percent).

The Vice Presidents Who Cast the Fewest Tie-Breaking Votes in the Senate:

At the other end of the spectrum, 12 Vice Presidents cast no tie-breaking votes during their terms of office (though some of those terms were vanishingly brief):

JOHN TYLER (March 4–April 4, 1841)

WILLIAM KING (March 4–April 18, 1853)

ANDREW JOHNSON (March 4–April 15, 1861)

THOMAS HENDRICKS (March 4–November 25, 1885)

THEODORE ROOSEVELT (March 4–September 14, 1901)

CHARLES FAIRBANKS (March 4, 1905–March 4, 1909): the first to serve a complete four-year term without casting a tie-breaking vote (there were 212 recorded votes during his four years in office)

CALVIN COOLIDGE (March 4, 1921–August 2, 1923)

LYNDON JOHNSON (January 20, 1961–November 22, 1963)

GERALD FORD (December 6, 1973–August 9, 1974)

NELSON ROCKEFELLER (December 19, 1974–January 20, 1977)

DAN QUAYLE (January 20, 1989–January 20, 1993): the second to serve a complete four-year term with no tie-breaking votes (there were 1,188 recorded votes during his four years in office)

JOE BIDEN (January 20, 2009–): the first to serve more than four years with no tie-breaking votes (as of 2015, there have been 2,178 votes during his time in office)

Senate Tie-Breaking Votes by Party:

1. DEMOCRATS. Vice Presidents who were members of the Democratic Party served 70 years, 8 months and, in that time, cast 84 tie-breaking votes (an average of 0.10 per month, or 0.43 percent of 19,751 recorded votes).

2. REPUBLICANS. Republican Vice Presidents served 75 years, 11 months and, in that time, cast 73 tie-breaking votes (an average of 0.08 per month, or 0.32 percent of 23,143 recorded votes).

3. DEMOCRAT-REPUBLICANS. Democrat-Republicans were in office for 35 years, 10 months straight (from the time Thomas Jefferson took office on March 4, 1797, until John Calhoun resigned, on December 28, 1832). In that time, they cast 55 tie-breaking votes (an average of 0.13 per month, or 1.69 percent of 3,254 recorded votes).

4. FEDERALISTS. John Adams was the only Federalist Vice President, and he cast 29 tie-breaking votes in nearly eight years in office (an average of 0.31 per month, or 9.15 percent of 317 recorded votes).

5. WHIGS. There were four Whig Presidents, only two Vice Presidents (they both succeeded to the Presidency when their Presidents died). In 17 months of Whig Vice Presidents, they cast three tie-breaking votes (an average of 0.18 per month; there were 1,984 recorded votes during the eight years Whigs were President).

52. Electoral Vote Counters

One of the Vice President's duties, as President of the Senate, is to preside over the counting of the electoral ballots to determine the next President and Vice President. The 12th Amendment reads, in part: "The Electors shall meet in their respective states and vote by ballot for President and Vice-President . . . and they shall make distinct lists of all persons voted for as President, and of all persons voted for as Vice-President . . . which lists they shall sign and certify, and transmit sealed to the seat of the government of the United States, directed to the President of the Senate;—the President of the Senate shall, in the presence of the Senate and House of Representatives, open all the certificates and the votes shall then be counted . . ." Which has lead, several times in the country's history, to some potentially awkward days in Congress.

On February 11, 1801, Vice President Thomas Jefferson opened the ballots (which, before the adoption of the 12th Amendment, did not differentiate between candidates for President and for Vice President). At that time, each state chose its own election day, and voting lasted from April to October. South Carolina was the last state to vote and broke the at-that-point electoral tie in favor of the Democrat-Republicans, giving the election to Jefferson and his Vice Presidential running mate, Aaron Burr. But the Democrat-Republicans neglected to have one of their electors abstain from voting for Burr, so both Jefferson and Burr wound up with 73 electoral votes each. At that time, Article II, Section 1 of the Constitution read in part, "The Person having the greatest Number of Votes shall be the President, if such Number be a Majority of the whole Number of Electors appointed; and if there be more than one who have such Majority, and have an equal Number of Votes, then the House of Representatives shall immediately chuse by Ballot one of them for President . . . after the Choice of the President, the Person having the greatest Number of Votes of the Electors shall be the Vice President. But if there should remain two or more who have equal Votes, the Senate shall chuse from them by Ballot the Vice President."

The tie vote thus threw the election to the House of Representatives, and while the Democrat-Republicans controlled the incoming House, 68 seats to 38, they hadn't taken office yet. The outgoing House, elected in 1798, was controlled by the Federalists, 60 seats to 46, and they were the ones on whom the choice devolved. It was common knowledge that Jefferson was the candidate for President and Burr for Vice President, but many of the Federalists controlling the House were so opposed to Jefferson that they voted for Burr, repeatedly. Over the week from February 11 to 17, the House voted 35 times, with identical results each time, and Burr never bowing out (which caused his split with Jefferson that denied him renomination in 1804). Finally, on the 36th ballot, several Federalists capitulated, casting blank ballots instead of voting for Burr, which tipped the scales enough to allow Jefferson the victory.

On February 13, 1805, following the election of 1804, Vice President Aaron Burr had to count the ballots that forced him out of office. Following his break with Thomas Jefferson four years previously and the adoption of the 12th Amendment—which provided for the President and Vice President to run as a team—Jefferson had dropped Burr from the ticket in favor of George Clinton. Burr thus counted the ballots that elected his successor to the job.

On February 8, 1809, following the election of 1808, Vice President George Clinton counted the ballots that returned him to his office for another four-year term, while swapping out President Jefferson (who was retiring after eight years) for President James Madison.

The election of 1828 resembled that of two decades earlier, in that Vice President John C. Calhoun stayed in his post while the President changed. In 1824, the only functional party was the Democrat-Republicans, and the four candidates who received votes were all of the same party. John Quincy Adams finally was elected President by the House of Representatives, while

John C. Calhoun had won an easy majority in the general election for Vice President. By 1828, the Democrat-Republicans were splitting into two parties. Andrew Jackson was the nominee of the Democrats and chose sitting Vice President Calhoun as his running mate. President Adams was the nominee of the National Republicans (later to be known as the Whigs) and chose Secretary of the Treasury Richard Rush as his running mate. On February 11, 1829, Vice President Calhoun opened the ballots that turned Adams out of office, but kept him in his office, while electing Jackson as the new President.

On February 8, 1837, Martin Van Buren became the first Vice President since Thomas Jefferson in 1801 to preside over the counting of the ballots that promoted him from Vice President to President. Unlike Jefferson's election, however, Van Buren had won an easy majority of the electoral votes, taking 170 of the 294 cast, with four others splitting the remainder. What was in dispute in this election was the Vice Presidential balloting. Virginia's 23 electors had all been pledged to Van Buren and his running mate, Richard Mentor Johnson, and while they did vote for Van Buren, they refused to vote for Johnson, leaving him one vote short of the 148-vote majority required to elect him. Under the terms of the 12th Amendment, the Vice Presidential election was immediately kicked to the Senate, where it had to decide between Johnson and Francis Granger. Johnson easily won that election, 33 to 16.

In the election of 1840, the Democrats refused to renominate Vice President Johnson (although President Van Buren was their choice for another term). Van Buren was unwilling to drop Johnson from his ticket, so as a compromise, the party chose to not nominate any Vice Presidential candidate, and though Johnson campaigned for reelection, the Democrats lost, and on February 10, 1841, Johnson wound up counting the ballots that turned him and Van Buren out of office in favor of Whigs William Henry Harrison and John Tyler.

On February 13, 1861, Vice President John C. Breckinridge—who had been the Southern Democrats' nominee for President—announced his defeat in the Presidential election to Republican Abraham Lincoln (Breckinridge came in third in the popular vote and a distant second in the Electoral College). On March 4, Breckinridge swore in his successor, Hannibal Hamlin, as the new Vice President. Hamlin then swore in the newly elected Senators, including Breckinridge, who would now represent Kentucky. His time in the Senate, however, was brief. Following Lincoln's inauguration, Southern states began seceding, and on April 12, Confederate troops fired on Fort Sumter, kicking off the Civil War. Kentucky maintained neutrality until September, and by the middle of that month, Breckinridge was on the run. In early October, he publicly announced that he was joining the Confederate Army. He was indicted for treason on November 6, and the Senate declared him a traitor on December 2. The resolution read, "Whereas John C. Breckinridge, a member of this body from the State of Kentucky, has joined the enemies of his country, and is now in arms against the government he had sworn to support: Therefore—Resolved, That said John C. Breckinridge, the traitor, be, and he hereby is, expelled from the Senate." It was adopted by a vote of 36 to 0 on December 4.

In the election of 1864, President Lincoln chose to drop Vice President Hannibal Hamlin in favor of Southern Democrat Andrew Johnson, who had stayed loyal to the Union. Lincoln's reelection, during the summer, was by no means assured, and he made the political calculation that his "National Union" ticket, including a Democrat, was his best chance of winning. The tide of the war turned late in the year, and Lincoln was handily reelected with Johnson. On February 8, 1865, Hamlin was forced to count the ballots that turned him out of office in favor of Johnson (who would then serve a scant six weeks as Vice President before succeeding to the Presidency).

In 1870, Vice President Shuyler Colfax announced he would not run for political office in 1872. In 1872, the Republican Convention made that official, choosing Henry Wilson over Colfax (who had apparently changed his mind). Colfax, however, had also been tarred by the Crédit Mobilier scandal, so he was no longer a viable candidate. On February 12, 1873, he was forced to count the ballots that returned Ulysses Grant to the Presidency and made Wilson his successor.

In the election of 1892, President Benjamin Harrison and Vice President Levi Morton lost to former President Grover Cleveland his newest Vice Presidential running mate Adlai Stevenson. Thus, on February 8, 1893, Morton became the only Vice President to announce the election of a former President to the office. He also had to announce his own defeat.

In 1940, Vice President John Nance Garner decided to run for President. Later that year, President Franklin Roosevelt announced his break with tradition and his decision to run for a third term. Roosevelt dropped Garner from his ticket, choosing instead Secretary of Agriculture Henry A. Wallace. On January 6, 1941, Garner announced the reelection of his President and his own departure from office in favor of his successor, Wallace.

In 1944, his Democratic Party forced President Roosevelt to drop Vice President Wallace from the ticket for his fourth Presidential campaign, and he chose instead Senator Harry Truman. Thus, Wallace, like Garner before him, on January 6, 1945, wound up announcing Roosevelt's reelection and the election of his own successor.

In the election of 1960, Vice President Richard Nixon ran a hard and very close, but ultimately unsuccessful campaign for the Presidency. Senator John Kennedy won the popular vote by 0.17 percent (the closest vote margin in the twentieth century), though he took the electoral vote 303 to 219. Thus, Nixon was forced to announce his own defeat for the Presidency on January 6, 1961, as he also announced Senator Lyndon Johnson's elevation to President of the Senate.

In the election of 1968, Vice President Hubert Humphrey felt what Nixon had eight years earlier. As the sitting Vice President running for President, he wound up losing a very close election (Humphrey lost the popular vote by 0.7 percent) to former Vice President Richard Nixon. But then, as President of the Senate, on January 6, 1969, Humphrey became the only one to announce the election of a former Vice President to the Presidency.

In 1976, for the first time, a person who had not been elected Vice President in the previous election was the President of the Senate who announced the electoral vote totals. The 25th Amendment had been adopted, and under its terms, first Gerald Ford and then Nelson Rockefeller had been appointed Vice President. But in the election of 1976, now-President Ford had dropped Rockefeller from his ticket, choosing instead Senator Bob Dole as his running mate. Rockefeller therefore, on January 6, 1977, became the first to announce the defeat of his President and the election of his own successor (Vice President Walter Mondale) without himself having lost an election.

On January 4, 1989, for the first time since 1837, the sitting Vice President, George H.W. Bush, was able to announce his own election as President.

On the night of November 7, 2000, Vice President Al Gore was declared the winner of the Presidential election. Then Voter News Service (a consortium formed by six news organizations to collect and share exit polling data) walked back their announcement and instead declared Texas Governor George W. Bush the winner. Then they modified their call once again, announcing that the results were too close to call in Florida. Unfortunately, announcing those results tainted the public's view of the election before all the ballots had been counted. Those early calls also marked the downfall and eventual disbandment of Voter News Service. The public had become used to having results instantaneously and to having the ballot count to the exact number, but the count in Florida proved so close that it automatically triggered a recount, and the inexactitude of ballot counting was thrust to the forefront of the public's awareness. Several recounts, partial recounts, lawsuits, and court decisions resulted in the Supreme Court stepping in to rule—in *Bush v. Gore*, announced on December 12, 2000—that the recounting should cease immediately, at a point where Bush was ahead, and Florida's electoral votes went to Bush, along with the election.

On January 6, 2001, during the joint session of Congress to count the electoral vote, 20 members of the House of Representatives each objected to the electoral votes from Florida, but their objections were deemed out of order, pursuant to the Electoral Count Act of 1887 (itself adopted in the aftermath of the electoral confusion in 1876, in which a special commission of Senators, Representatives, and Supreme Court Justices was appointed to settle the disputes over the electoral votes from Florida, Louisiana, Oregon, and South Carolina). Vice President Gore, sitting as President of the Senate, therefore presided over the counting of the electoral votes that gave the Presidency to George W. Bush.

This was the fourth election in which the eventual winner did not win a plurality of the popular vote (after John Quincy Adams in 1824, Rutherford Hayes in 1876, and Benjamin Harrison in 1888).

53. The Vice Presidents Who Ran For, but Did Not Win, the Presidency

This list does not include Vice Presidents who became President and then lost their bids for reelection.

The first three Vice Presidents—John Adams, Thomas Jefferson, and Aaron Burr—all ran for office before the adoption of the 12th Amendment. That Amendment, adopted in 1804, changed the manner in which Vice Presidents are chosen. Originally, the candidate who received the second greatest number of electoral votes became the Vice President, but the tie between Jefferson and Burr in 1800 (each received 73 electoral votes) pointed out the need to change this provision of the Constitution. The 12th Amendment provided for Presidential and Vice Presidential candidates to run, and be elected, as a team.

1. GEORGE CLINTON. Clinton was elected Vice President in 1804, and was again the Democrat-Republican Vice Presidential nominee in 1808. However, Clinton disagreed with the caucus nominating process, and he allowed his supporters to campaign for him for President. As a Presidential candidate, however, Clinton was only viable in his home state of New York, where he won 6 of the 19 electoral votes (which was his total for the election). He was reelected Vice President and served until his death on April 20, 1812.

2. JOHN C. BRECKINRIDGE was the first sitting Vice President since Martin Van Buren to run for the Presidency, in 1857. Unlike Van Buren, Breckinridge lost. After serving under James Buchanan during his one term, Breckinridge ran under the National Democrat banner for President, nominated by the Southern Democrats who'd left the national convention that ultimately nominated Stephen Douglas. Breckinridge placed third in

the election of 1860, losing to Abraham Lincoln and Douglas, but winning more votes than John Bell, the nominee of the Constitutional Union Party. After his loss, Breckinridge returned to the Senate, but when Kentucky did not secede, Breckinridge joined the Confederacy as a General and, toward the end of the Civil War, as Secretary of War. After the Confederacy's surrender, Breckinridge took refuge abroad, returning under the general amnesty of 1868. He died in 1875 at the age of 54, the second-youngest Vice Presidential death ever.

3. HENRY A. WALLACE was Franklin Delano Roosevelt's second Vice President (1941–45). His successor, Harry S Truman, succeeded to the Presidency upon Roosevelt's death in April 1945. In the election of 1948, the Communist Party, as well as left-leaning Democrats who were unhappy with Truman's policies toward the USSR, convened as the Progressive Party and nominated Wallace for President. Wallace placed fourth in the election, behind Truman, Republican Thomas E. Dewey, and Dixiecrat (southern Democrat) Strom Thurmond.

4. RICHARD M. NIXON was the first sitting Vice President since John C. Breckinridge—100 years earlier—to run for President. Unlike Breckinridge, Nixon was the sole nominee of his Party, but he lost the very close election of 1960 to Democrat John F. Kennedy. Eight years later, Nixon became the only former Vice President to be elected President.

5. HUBERT H. HUMPHREY was Lyndon Johnson's Vice President (1965–69), and he got the Democratic Party's nomination after Johnson announced he would not be a candidate for another term. Humphrey lost a close race to former Vice President Richard M. Nixon in 1968, with American Independent candidate George Wallace taking more than 13 percent of the popular vote and 46 of the 538 electoral votes.

6. WALTER F. MONDALE, who was Jimmy Carter's Vice President (1977–81), was the Democratic nominee for President in 1984. Unfortunately for him, he was running against Ronald Reagan's reelection juggernaut,

during which Reagan won 59 percent of the popular vote and 525 of the 538 electoral votes. Mondale was later appointed Ambassador to Japan by President Bill Clinton.

7. ALBERT GORE, JR., who was Bill Clinton's Vice President (1993–2001) ran for the Presidency in 2000 against Republican George W. Bush. Gore won the popular vote, but several lawsuits over the recounting of ballots in Florida were eventually decided by the Supreme Court in Bush's favor, giving Bush the election.

The following three former Vice Presidents served terms as Presidents before retiring and then, later, ran again for the Presidency but lost.

MARTIN VAN BUREN, who had been Vice President (1833–37) and then was elected President (1837–41), ran on the Free Soil ticket in the election of 1848, losing to Whig Zachary Taylor and coming in third behind Democrat Lewis Cass. Van Buren won no electoral votes in this election.

MILLARD FILLMORE, who had been Vice President (1849–50) and then succeeded to the Presidency (1850–53) upon Zachary Taylor's death, was the American, or Know-Nothing, Party's candidate for President in 1856. He came in third, behind Democratic winner James Buchanan and Republican second-place candidate John C. Frémont.

THEODORE ROOSEVELT, who had been Vice President (1901), succeeded to the Presidency upon William McKinley's death and then won his own term as President (1904); he retired in 1909 making way for his hand-picked successor, William Howard Taft. Roosevelt and Taft split during the latter's term of office, and Roosevelt returned to try to take back the Republican nomination in 1912. He didn't get the nomination and left the party, forming his own Progressive, or Bull Moose, Party. Under that banner, he came in second to Democrat Woodrow Wilson, forcing Taft down to third place in the election of 1912.

54. *The Only Vice President to Be Inaugurated Outside the United States of America*

WILLIAM RUFUS DEVANE KING was the only national officeholder to be inaugurated outside the United States of America. He was born on April 7, 1786, in North Carolina, and served in the House of Representatives from 1811 to 1816, when he resigned to serve as Secretary of the US Legation at Naples, Italy. He moved with the legation to St. Petersburg, Russia, and then returned to the United States in 1818. He moved to Alabama and was a delegate to the convention that organized the state government. Following Alabama's admission as a state in 1819, he was elected as the state's first Senator and then reelected four times. He represented Alabama in the Senate from December 14, 1819, to April 15, 1844, when he resigned to become US Minister to France (where he served for two years). He returned home in 1846, and then was appointed to fill a vacant Senate seat on July 1, 1848 (to which he was eventually elected). He resigned that seat on December 20, 1852. During his 28 years in the Senate, he served as President pro tempore from July 1836 to March 1841 (at the time, Presidents pro tempore were chosen each time the Vice President was absent, so he was chosen for the position 10 times during this period), and again from May 1850 to December 1852 (three distinct periods). From July 11, 1850, until he left the position on December 20, 1852, King was next in line for the Presidency (this was the period after Millard Fillmore had succeeded to the Presidency, and there was no Vice President).

King was elected Vice President with Franklin Pierce in the election of 1852, but he was suffering from terminal tuberculosis at the time. Following his resignation from the Senate, he went to Cuba in hopes that the change of climate would improve his condition. By a special act of Congress, in recognition of King's long service in the government, he was permitted to take the oath of office on foreign soil and did so on March 24, 1853. He returned to his Alabama plantation, "King's Bend," on April 16, 1853, and died two days later.

King was buried on his plantation, but his body was moved in 1882 to Live Oak Cemetery in Selma, Alabama, the town he co-founded.

When he first took office as a Representative from North Carolina, he had not yet reached his 25th birthday, and thus, per Article I, Section 2 of the Constitution, he was ineligible to serve. In the early days of the Republic, however, adherence to this age limitation was not as strict. Several Congressmen, in the early days, were younger than 25. The youngest ever was William Charles Cole Claiborne of Tennessee, who was elected to the fifth Congress (1797–99) and began his service at the age of 22.

55. Elections in Which None of the Presidential or Vice Presidential Candidates Had Been President or Vice President

There-quarters of the quadrennial elections have boasted at least one major party candidate who was currently or had previously been President or Vice President. The election of 2008 was one of the minority. 2012 saw President Obama and Vice President Biden running for reelection. For the election of 2016, there are only seven retired eligible Presidents and Vice Presidents: Vice President Joe Biden (2009–); Vice President Dick Cheney (2001–09); Vice President Al Gore (1993–2001; lost the election of 2000); President George H.W. Bush (lost his bid for reelection in 1992; he'll be 92 in 2016); Vice President Dan Quayle (1989–93); President Jimmy Carter (lost his bid for reelection in 1980; he'll be 92 in 2016); and Vice President Walter Mondale (lost the election of 1984; he'll be 88 in 2016). The youngest of them, Al Gore, will be 68 in 2016.

In every election, there have been more than two candidates, but the few times the third-party candidates were former Presidents or Vice Presidents, they were running against incumbents, so those elections do not appear on this list.

The election of 2008 was the last to see no Presidents or Vice Presidents running. Democratic Senator Barack Obama and Senator Joe Biden defeated Republican Senator John McCain and Alaska Governor Sarah Palin.

The election of 1952 saw Republican General Dwight D. Eisenhower and Senator Richard M. Nixon defeat Democrat Adlai E. Stevenson and John J. Sparkman.

The election of 1920 had no Presidents or Vice Presidents running, but three of the four major party candidates would later serve as President. Republican Warren G. Harding won the election with Vice Presidential candidate Calvin Coolidge, who would succeed upon Harding's death in 1923. Democrat James M. Cox headed the losing ticket with Vice Presidential candidate Franklin D. Roosevelt, who would later win four elections as President (1932, 1936, 1940, and 1944).

The election of 1908 saw Republicans William Howard Taft and James Sherman defeat Democrats William Jennings Bryan and John Kern. This was Bryan's third losing run for the Presidency (after 1896 and 1900).

In the election of 1896, Republican William McKinley was elected with Garret Hobart as his number two, defeating William Jennings Bryan (in his first run for the Presidency) and Arthur Sewall.

The election of 1884, the first of three in which Democrat Grover Cleveland would run (winning, losing, and then winning), saw him and Thomas Hendricks (who had run in 1876) defeat Republicans James Blaine and John Logan.

The election of 1880 was the second of three in a row with inexperienced candidates. Republicans James A. Garfield and Chester A. Arthur defeated Democrats Winfield Hancock and William English.

The election of 1876 saw Republicans Rutherford B. Hayes and William A. Wheeler defeat Democrats Samuel J. Tilden and Thomas Hendricks (who would win the Vice Presidency eight years later).

In the election of 1868, Republicans Ulysses S. Grant and Shuyler Colfax defeated Democrats Horatio Seymour and Francis Blair.

The election of 1852 saw Democrat Franklin Pierce and William R. King defeat Whig Winfield Scott and William Alexander Graham.

The election of 1844 saw Democrat James Knox Polk and George M. Dallas defeat Whig Henry Clay and Theodore Frelinghuysen. Though Clay had never been President or Vice President, this was his third election as a Presidential candidate (following 1824 and 1832).

The election of 1824 was more of an electoral free-for-all. In the last election before political parties started to exert major influence, all four major candidates were Democrat-Republicans, and none received a majority of the electoral votes, so the House of Representatives chose the victor. The four candidates who received electoral votes were: eventual victor John Quincy Adams (84 electoral votes), Andrew Jackson (99), Henry Clay (37), and William Harris Crawford (41). The candidates who received electoral votes for Vice President were John C. Calhoun (182), Nathan Sanford (30), Nathaniel Macon (24), Andrew Jackson (13), Martin Van Buren (9, he was elected Vice President in 1832), and Henry Clay (2).

The election of 1816 saw Democrat-Republicans James Monroe and Daniel D. Tompkins defeat Federalist Rufus King and his running mates (who varied from state to state): Robert Goodloe Harper, John Eager Howard, John Marshall, and James Ross.

The election of 1789, of course, couldn't have any experienced candidates, because it chose the first President. George Washington was unanimously elected, with John Adams elected Vice President.

CABINET MEMBERS

The United States Cabinet (also known as the President's Cabinet or just the Cabinet) is composed of the most senior appointed officers of the executive branch of the federal government of the United States. Its existence dates back to the first President, George Washington, who appointed a Cabinet of four people (Secretary of State Thomas Jefferson, Secretary of the Treasury Alexander Hamilton, Secretary of War Henry Knox, and Attorney General Edmund Randolph) to advise and assist him. Cabinet officers are nominated by the President and confirmed (or rejected) by the Senate.

Article II, Section 2 of the Constitution says that the President "shall nominate, and by and with the Advice and Consent of the Senate, shall appoint Ambassadors, other public Ministers and Consuls, Judges of the Supreme Court, and all other Officers of the United States, whose Appointments are not herein otherwise provided for, and which shall be established by Law: but the Congress may by Law vest the Appointment of such inferior Officers, as they think proper, in the President alone, in the Courts of Law, or in the Heads of Departments."

Article II also says the President can require "the Opinion, in writing, of the principal Officer in each of the executive Departments, upon any Subject relating to the Duties of their respective Offices." The Constitution did not spell out the names or number of Cabinet departments.

One of the few qualification restrictions on potential Cabinet members is, per Article I, "no person holding any office under the United States, shall be a member of either house during his continuance in office." In other words, Cabinet Secretaries cannot also be members of Congress.

The Cabinet itself is something of a legal fiction. It is not explicitly defined in the United States Code or the Code of Federal Regulations. There are, however, references to "cabinet-level officers" or "secretaries," which appear to refer to the heads of the "executive departments."

A law adopted in 1967 prohibits federal officials from appointing family members to certain governmental posts, including the Cabinet. The law is an apparent response to John Kennedy's appointment of his brother Robert as Attorney General. But it doesn't prevent family members from serving together. John Kerry was appointed Secretary of State in February 2013. His younger brother, Cameron Kerry, had been General Counsel of the Department of Commerce since May 2009, and served as Acting Secretary of Commerce for the month of June 2013.

The Cabinet is also a part of the Presidential line of succession. Article II of the Constitution provides for the Vice President to step into the Presidency if there is no President. The 25th Amendment (proposed in 1965 and adopted in 1967) defines Presidential disability and the methods by which the Vice President may become President or Acting President. The Presidential Succession Act of 1947 (as amended in 1965, 1966, 1977, 1979, and 2006) sets the order of Presidential succession as: Vice President, Speaker of the House, President pro tempore of the Senate, and then the Cabinet Secretaries in the order in which their departments joined the Cabinet (with the exception that Defense replaced War and is third in the list). There has never been a need to use the order of succession beyond a Vice President stepping up to replace a President, but in order to maintain the continuity of government, there is always a "designated survivor" when events call for the attendance of the President, Vice President, the heads of Congress, and the Cabinet (such as State of the Union addresses): one Cabinet Secretary does not attend and remains elsewhere (presumably safely) should disaster strike the rest.

The Cabinet departments (former and current) are:

Name	Date First Secretary Took Office	Date Department Left the Cabinet	Number of Secretaries
State	September 26, 1789		68
Treasury	September 11, 1789		76
War	September 12, 1789	September 18, 1947 (became part of the Department of Defense)	56
Navy	June 18, 1798	September 18, 1947 (became part of the Department of Defense)	48
Defense	September 19, 1947		25
Justice (Secretary is the Attorney General)	September 26, 1789		83
Post Office (Secretary is the Postmaster General)	September 26, 1789 (joined the Cabinet March 9, 1829)	July 1, 1971	6 pre-Cabinet, 53 Cabinet level, 13 post-Cabinet
Interior	March 4, 1849		51
Agriculture	February 15, 1889		30
Commerce and Labor	February 18, 1903	March 4, 1913 (divided into two Cabinet departments)	4
Commerce	March 5, 1913		38
Labor	March 6, 1913		26
Health, Education, and Welfare (HEW)	April 11, 1953	September 27, 1979 (divided into two Cabinet departments)	13
Housing and Urban Development	January 18, 1966		16
Health and Human Services (HHS)	September 27, 1979		10
Education	November 30, 1979		9
Transportation	January 16, 1967		17
Energy	August 6, 1977		13
Veterans Affairs	March 15, 1989		8
Homeland Security	January 24, 2003		4

56. The Five Oldest Cabinet Secretaries

Ronald Reagan was the oldest President to take office, just weeks before his 70th birthday. But Cabinet Secretaries don't have to be voted in, so age is less of an impediment. The oldest people to take office in the Cabinet were:

1. HUGH MCCULLOCH. The 36th Secretary of the Treasury was 75 years, 328 days old on October 31, 1884, when he took office. He served for about four months, at the end of Chester Arthur's Administration. McCulloch had also been the 27th Secretary of the Treasury, serving under Abraham Lincoln and Andrew Johnson from 1865 to 1869. He was born on December 7, 1808.

2. LEWIS CASS. The 22nd Secretary of State was 74 years, 148 days old on March 6, 1857, when he took the post under James Buchanan (who had been Secretary of State himself). Cass, who'd been born October 9, 1782, resigned in December 1860. He had previously served as the 14th Secretary of War, from 1831 to 1836.

3. JOHN SHERMAN. The 35th Secretary of State was 73 years, 300 days old on March 6, 1897, when he took the job for William McKinley. Born May 10, 1823, he served in the post a little more than one year. He had previously been the 32nd Secretary of the Treasury for Rutherford Hayes (1877–81).

4. HENRY LEWIS STIMSON. The 54th Secretary of War was 72 years, 292 days old on July 10, 1940, when he took over as Franklin Roosevelt's third Secretary of War (he served into September 1945). Born September 21, 1867, Stimson had previously been the 45th Secretary of War from 1911 to 1913 (William Taft's second) and the 46th Secretary of State (1929–33, Herbert Hoover's term).

5. Philip Klutznick. The 25th Secretary of Commerce was the oldest first-time Cabinet Secretary. He was 72 years, 184 days old on January 9, 1980, when Jimmy Carter appointed him for his final year in office. Klutznick was born July 9, 1907.

The four other Secretaries appointed at 70 or more years of age were also first-timers:

Sixty-ninth Secretary of the Treasury Lloyd Millard Bentsen, Jr. He was 71 years, 343 days old on January 20, 1993, and served nearly two years under Bill Clinton.

Forty-fifth Secretary of the Treasury Franklin MacVeagh. He was 71 years, 106 days old on March 8, 1909, and served William Taft's entire term.

Forty-fifth Secretary of the Navy Claude Augustus Swanson. He was 70 years, 338 days old on March 4, 1933. Franklin Roosevelt's first Navy Secretary, he is the only one on this list to die in office (he died July 7, 1939).

Twenty-seventh Secretary of Commerce William Verity, Jr. He was 70 years, 266 days old on October 19, 1987, and served 15 months, ending Ronald Reagan's term and serving a week and a half into George H.W. Bush's.

57. The Five Youngest Cabinet Secretaries

The Presidential Succession Act of 1947 (with amendments) places the Cabinet Secretaries in line of succession to the Presidency, behind the Vice President, Speaker of the House, and President pro tempore of the Senate. But it also makes provision for skipping over those who are not otherwise eligible to be President. Thus, there is no age limit on Cabinet Secretaries.

1 (or 2). RICHARD RUSH. The eighth Attorney General was 33 years, 165 days old on February 10, 1814, when he became James Madison's third AG. He served in the post for just under four years (and was also Acting Secretary of State for six months in 1817). In 1825, John Quincy Adams appointed Rush the eighth Secretary of the Treasury.

2 (or 1). ALEXANDER HAMILTON. The first Secretary of the Treasury was born in the West Indies, but there's some question as to whether he was born in 1755 or 1757. Thus he was either the second-youngest or the youngest Cabinet member ever. He was either 34 years, 243 days or 32 years, 243 days old on September 11, 1789. He is known for having been killed in a duel with Aaron Burr in 1804, and his portrait appears on the $10 bill. His third son, James Alexander, was Acting Secretary of State for most of March 1829.

3. CAESAR A. RODNEY. The sixth Attorney General was 35 years, 16 days old on January 20, 1807. He served for just under five years and was later Ambassador to Argentina. He was the nephew of Caesar Rodney, who signed the Declaration of Independence.

4. OLIVER WOLCOTT, JR. The second Secretary of the Treasury was 35 years, 23 days old when he took office on February 3, 1795. He served just under six years.

5. ROBERT F. KENNEDY. The 64th Attorney General was 35 years, 61 days old on January 20, 1961, when his brother John Kennedy became the only President to appoint a sibling to his Cabinet. Attorney General Kennedy served into late 1964, and was assassinated four years later, while campaigning for the Democratic nomination for President.

Twenty-six more Cabinet Secretaries were under the age of 40 when they took office (the youngest President, Theodore Roosevelt, was 42 when he was sworn in). Seven of them were Secretaries of War; six Attorneys General; three Secretaries of the Navy; two each of Agriculture, Interior, and Transportation; and one each of Commerce, Treasury, HEW, and Postmaster General.

Gideon Granger was appointed Postmaster General by Thomas Jefferson prior to the position's elevation to a Cabinet-level post. He took office on November 28, 1801, at the age of 34 years, 132 days, which would rank him second or third on this list (depending on Alexander Hamilton's birth date). Granger served in that position for more than 12 years. He was the father of 10th Postmaster General Francis Granger, who served six months in 1841.

58. The Five Cabinet Secretaries Who Lived the Longest

1. EARL L. BUTZ. The 18th Secretary of Agriculture (1971–76) was born in Indiana on July 3, 1909. He served under Richard Nixon and Gerald Ford, his only term in the Cabinet. Butz died February 2, 2008, aged 98 years, 214 days.

2. W. WILLARD WIRTZ. The 10th Secretary of Labor (1962–69) was born March 14, 1912, in Illinois. He served under John Kennedy and Lyndon Johnson, and was the last surviving member of Kennedy's Cabinet when he died on April 24, 2010, aged 98 years, 41 days.

3. FRANKLIN MACVEAGH. The 45th Secretary of the Treasury (1909–13) was born November 22, 1837, in Pennsylvania. He served under William Taft and died July 6, 1934, aged 96 years, 226 days. His four-years-older brother, Wayne, was the 36th Attorney General for most of 1881.

4. JAMES D. HODGSON. The 12th Secretary of Labor (1970–73) died five days before his 96th birthday, on November 28, 2012. Born December 3, 1915, in Minnesota, he was also Gerald Ford's Ambassador to Japan (1974–77).

5. WILLIAM THADDEUS COLEMAN, JR. The fourth Secretary of Transportation (March 1975–January 1977), Coleman was born July 7, 1920, in Pennsylvania. He passed Otis R. Bowen (the 16th Secretary of Health and Human Services [1985–89], who died in 2013 at the age of 95 years, 67 days) on September 12, 2015, and will break Earl Butz's longevity record on February 6, 2019.

GEORGE PRATT SHULTZ is six months younger than Coleman. Born December 13, 1920, in New York, he was the 11th Secretary of Labor (January 1969–July 1970), the 62nd Secretary of the Treasury (June 1972–May 1974) and the 60th Secretary of State (July 1982–January 1989).

Thirty-one other Secretaries lived more than 90 years. They include six Secretaries of Commerce; five Secretaries of the Treasury; four Attorneys General; three Secretaries each of Defense and Interior; two Secretaries each of the Navy, Agriculture, and HEW; and one Secretary each of State, War, Commerce & Labor; and a Postmaster General. In addition, Elihu Root, who served as both Secretary of State and War, died eight days before his 92nd birthday.

59. The Five Cabinet Secretaries Who Died the Youngest

1. JOHN AARON RAWLINS. The 29th Secretary of War (March–September 1869) was born February 13, 1831, and died September 6, 1869, in office, of tuberculosis, at the age of 38 years, 159 days. He is buried in Arlington National Cemetery.

2. WILLIAM BRADFORD. The second Attorney General (January 1794–August 1795) was born September 14, 1755, and died, in office, on August 23, 1795, at the age of 39 years, 343 days.

3. THOMAS WALKER GILMER. The 15th Secretary of the Navy served only nine days. He was killed in the explosion aboard the USS *Princeton* that also took the lives of Secretary of State Abel Upshur and President John Tyler's soon-to-be father-in-law David Gardiner. Gilmer was born April 6, 1802, and died February 28, 1844, at the age of 41 years, 328 days.

4. ROBERT F. KENNEDY. The 64th Attorney General is the first one on this list who didn't die while in office. At the time of his assassination, June 6, 1968, he was a Senator representing New York and campaigning for the Democratic nomination for President. He had served his brother John Kennedy and Lyndon Johnson as Attorney General from January 1961 to September 1964. Born November 20, 1925, Kennedy was 42 years, 198 days old when he died.

5. JAMES COCHRAN DOBBIN. The 22nd Secretary of the Navy (1853–57) died five months after leaving office, on August 4, 1857. Born on January 17, 1814, he lived only 43 years, 199 days.

Five other Cabinet Secretaries died before the age of 50: fifth Attorney General John Breckinridge (46 years, 12 days); 52nd Attorney General Robert E. Hannegan (46 years, 98 days); 16th Attorney General Hugh Swinton Legaré (46 years, 169 days); 48th Secretary of State Edward Stettinius, Jr. (49 years, 9 days); and first Secretary of the Treasury Alexander Hamilton (either 49 years, 183 days or 47 years, 183 days).

60. The Five Cabinet Secretaries Who Lived the Longest after Leaving Office

Twelve members of the Cabinet have been retired from that post at least 40 years:

1–3. Three members of Lyndon Johnson's final Cabinet are still living, all having left office on January 20, 1969: first Secretary of Transportation ALAN STEPHENSON BOYD (born July 20, 1922, took office January 16, 1967), 66th Attorney General RAMSEY CLARK (born December 18, 1927, took office March 10, 1967), and 58th Postmaster General W. MARVIN WATSON (born June 6, 1924, took office April 22, 1968).

4. NICHOLAS KATZENBACH. The 65th Attorney General (January 28, 1965–November 28, 1966) had previously been Deputy and Acting Attorney General and was Under Secretary of State until the end of Lyndon Johnson's term of office. Katzenbach was born January 17, 1922, and exceeded George Bancroft's record on April 7, 2011. Katzenbach died on May 8, 2012, setting the record at 45 years, 162 days.

5. GEORGE BANCROFT. The 17th Secretary of the Navy (March 11, 1845–September 9, 1846) was born in October 1800. After leaving the Cabinet, he lived another 44 years, 130 days. During that time, he was Ambassador to England (1846–49) and later to Berlin (1867–74). He died January 17, 1891.

The others with exceedingly long retirements include:

RICHARD RUSH. The eighth Attorney General (February 10, 1814–November 12, 1817) was only 33 years old when he took office. After leaving that post, he was the eighth Secretary of State (1825–29). He died on July 30, 1859, having been a retired Attorney General for 41 years, 260 days.

JAMES DONALD CAMERON. The 32nd Secretary of War (May 22, 1876–March 4, 1877) was retired from the job for 41 years, 179 days. He died August 30, 1918.

ROBERT TODD LINCOLN. The 35th Secretary of War (March 5, 1881–March 4, 1885) was the son of President Abraham Lincoln; he was 21 when his father was assassinated. Secretary Lincoln joined James Garfield's Cabinet before his 38th birthday (and was with Garfield when he was shot that July). Robert also served as Ambassador to the UK from 1889 to 1893, and died July 26, 1926, 41 years, 144 days after retiring from the Cabinet.

ROBERT STRANGE MCNAMARA. The eighth Secretary of Defense (January 21, 1961–February 29, 1968) became the fifth President of the World Bank (April 1968–June 1981). His tenure there was the second longest. McNamara died July 6, 2009, at the age of 93. He had been retired from the Cabinet for 41 years, 128 days.

STEWART LEE UDALL. The 37th Secretary of the Interior (January 21, 1961–January 20, 1969). He had previously been a member of the House of Representatives for six years. His brother, Morris, served 30 years in the House. His son, Tom (representing New Mexico), and his nephew, Mark (representing Colorado), both served in the House from 1999 to 2009, and both were elected to the Senate in the election of 2008. Stewart died March 20, 2010, at the age of 90, having been retired from the Cabinet for 41 years, 59 days.

JAMES RUDOLPH GARFIELD. The 23rd Secretary of the Interior (March 5, 1907–March 5, 1909) was the son of President James Abram Garfield; he was 15 when his father was assassinated. Secretary Garfield joined Theodore Roosevelt's Cabinet when he was 41 and died March 24, 1950, having been retired from the Cabinet 41 years, 19 days.

OVETA CULP HOBBY. The first Secretary of Health, Education, and Welfare (April 11, 1953–July 31, 1955), she had previously been the first commanding officer of the Women's Army Corps (with the rank of Colonel). She resigned from the Cabinet to care for her ailing husband, William P. Hobby, the former Governor of Texas. She died August 16, 1995, 40 years, 16 days after leaving the Cabinet, at the age of 90.

61. The Cabinet Secretaries
Who Died in Office

Of the 634 Cabinet Secretaries confirmed by the Senate, 22 of them (3.5 percent) died in office. This number compares to 18.6 percent (8 of 43) Presidents and 14.9 percent (7 of 47) Vice Presidents.

WILLIAM BRADFORD. The second Attorney General (January 27, 1794–August 23, 1795), he died three weeks before his 40th birthday.

JOHN BRECKINRIDGE. The fifth Attorney General (August 7, 1805–December 14, 1806), he died two weeks after his 46th birthday. His grandson, John C., would later be the 14th Vice President.

HUGH SWINTON LEGARÉ. The 16th Attorney General (September 13, 1841–June 30, 1843), he was 46 years old.

ABEL P. UPSHUR. The 15th Secretary of State (July 24, 1843–February 28, 1844) died in an explosion aboard the USS *Princeton* at which President John Tyler was present, but uninjured. He had previously served as the 13th Secretary of the Navy (October 11, 1841–July 23, 1843). He was 53 years old.

THOMAS WALKER GILMER. The 15th Secretary of the Navy (February 19–28, 1844), he, too, died in the explosion aboard the USS *Princeton*. He was a month shy of his 42nd birthday.

DANIEL WEBSTER. The 19th Secretary of State (July 23, 1850–October 24, 1852), he had previously been the 14th Secretary of State (March 6, 1841–May 8, 1843). He was 70 years old.

AARON V. BROWN. The 17th Postmaster General (March 6, 1857–March 8, 1859), he was 63 years old.

JOHN AARON RAWLINS. The 29th Secretary of War (March 13–September 6, 1869), he died aged 38 years, 159 days.

TIMOTHY O. HOWE. The 30th Postmaster General (December 20, 1881–March 25, 1883), he was 67 years old.

CHARLES JAMES FOLGER. The 34th Secretary of the Treasury (November 14, 1881–September 4, 1884), he was 66 years old.

WILLIAM WINDOM. The 39th Secretary of the Treasury (March 7, 1889–January 29, 1891), he had also served as the 33rd Secretary of the Treasury (March 8–November 13, 1881). He was 63 years old.

WALTER Q. GRESHAM. The 33rd Secretary of State (March 7, 1893–May 28, 1895) had previously been the 31st Postmaster General (April 3, 1883–September 4, 1884) and the 35th Secretary of the Treasury (September 5–October 30, 1884). He was 63 years old.

HENRY C. PAYNE. The 40th Postmaster General (January 9, 1902–October 4, 1904), he was 60 years old.

JOHN HAY. The 37th Secretary of State (September 30, 1898–July 1, 1905), he was 66 years old.

HENRY C. WALLACE. The seventh Secretary of Agriculture (March 5, 1921–October 25, 1924), he was 58 years old. His son, Henry A., would follow in his footsteps as the 11th Secretary of Agriculture (March 4, 1933–September 4, 1940) and then be elected the 33rd Vice President (1941–45), before finally being appointed the 10th Secretary of Commerce (March 2, 1945–September 20, 1946).

JAMES WILLIAM GOOD. The 50th Secretary of War (March 6–November 18, 1929), he was 63 years old.

GEORGE HENRY DERN. The 52nd Secretary of War (March 4, 1933–August 27, 1936), he died 12 days before his 64th birthday.

CLAUDE AUGUSTUS SWANSON. The 45th Secretary of the Navy (March 4, 1933–July 7, 1939), he was 77 years old.

WILLIAM FRANKLIN KNOX. The 47th Secretary of the Navy (July 11, 1940–April 28, 1944), he was 70 years old.

LEWIS B. SCHWELLENBACH. The fifth Secretary of Labor (July 1, 1945–June 10, 1948), he was 53 years old.

HOWARD M. BALDRIGE, JR. The 26th Secretary of Commerce (January 20, 1981–July 25, 1987), he died in a horseback-riding accident at the age of 64.

RON BROWN. The 30th Secretary of Commerce (January 22, 1993–April 3, 1996), he died in an airplane crash in Croatia at the age of 54.

62. The Five Cabinet Secretaries Who Died the Soonest after Leaving Office

Sixteen Cabinet Secretaries died less than a year after leaving office.

1. JOHN FOSTER DULLES. The 52nd Secretary of State (January 21, 1953–April 22, 1959) left office because of illness. There is still some mystery surrounding his death, whether he fell, jumped, or was pushed off a high floor in the military hospital in which he'd been staying since leaving office, ostensibly undergoing treatment for depression. He died May 24, 1959, aged 71, only 32 days after leaving office.

2. JAMES VINCENT FORRESTAL. The first Secretary of Defense (September 19, 1947–March 19, 1949), he'd also been the 48th (and last Cabinet-level) Secretary of the Navy (from May 19, 1944). Born in 1892, he died May 22, 1949, 64 days after leaving office.

3. FREDERICK FRELINGHUYSEN. The 29th Secretary of State (December 19, 1881–March 6, 1885), he died May 20, 1885, aged 67, and 75 days after leaving office.

4. ALEXANDER JAMES DALLAS. The sixth Secretary of the Treasury (October 6, 1814–October 21, 1816), he'd been born in Jamaica. Dallas died January 16, 1817, having been retired 87 days. He didn't live to see his son, George Mifflin Dallas, serve as Vice President from 1845 to 1849.

5. WILLIAM LEARNED MARCY. The 21st Secretary of State (March 7, 1853–March 6, 1857), he'd also been the 20th Secretary of War (March 6, 1845–March 4, 1849). He died in his 70th year, on July 4, 1857, 120 days after leaving the Cabinet for the final time.

The 11 others who enjoyed less than one year of retirement include:

Seventh Postmaster General WILLIAM T. BARRY: served March 9, 1829–April 30, 1835, died August 30, 1835.

Fifty-first Secretary of the Treasury WILLIAM HARTMAN WOODIN: served March 5–December 31, 1933, died May 3, 1934.

Twenty-second Secretary of the Navy JAMES COCHRAN DOBBIN: served March 8, 1853–March 4, 1857, died August 4, 1857, at the age of 43.

Sixth Secretary of Labor MAURICE J. TOBIN: served August 13, 1948–January 20, 1953, died July 19, 1953.

Thirteenth Secretary of the Navy ABEL PARKER UPSHUR: October 11, 1841–July 23, 1843; he left that post to become the 15th Secretary of State and then died in that office on February 28, 1844, in the explosion aboard the USS *Princeton*.

Thirteenth Secretary of State JOHN FORSYTH: served July 1, 1834–March 3, 1841, died October 21, 1841.

Third Secretary of Labor WILLIAM N. DOAK: served December 9, 1930–March 4, 1933, died October 23, 1933.

Second Secretary of Agriculture JEREMIAH M. RUSK: served March 6, 1889–March 6, 1893, died November 21, 1893.

Thirty-seventh Secretary of the Treasury DANIEL MANNING: served March 8, 1885–March 31, 1887, died December 24, 1887.

Forty-eighth Secretary of War JOHN WINGATE WEEKS: served March 5, 1921–October 13, 1925, died July 12, 1926. His son, Charles Sinclair Weeks, was the 13th Secretary of Commerce (1953–58).

Thirteenth Attorney General FELIX GRUNDY: served July 5, 1838–January 10, 1840, died December 19, 1840.

63. The Most Popular States for Cabinet Secretaries to Be Born

The Senate has confirmed more than 600 Cabinet Secretaries in the 225 years since the Constitution was adopted. And while some concentration of birthplaces is to be expected, it may be surprising just how concentrated the birth states of Cabinet Secretaries are. Indeed, the top five states account for more than 40 percent of all Cabinet Secretaries.

1. NEW YORK is the birth state of 85 Secretaries. That's 12.5 percent, or one in every eight Cabinet Secretaries born in New York. The New Yorkers include 12 each Secretaries of State and Secretaries of the Treasury; nine each Attorneys General and Postmasters General; eight Secretaries of War; five Navy; four each Commerce, Labor, and Housing and Urban Development; three Defense; two each Interior, Agriculture, Commerce & Labor, HEW, Veterans Affairs, and Homeland Security; one each HHS, Education, and Energy. New Yorkers were the first Secretaries of Defense, Agriculture, Commerce & Labor, Commerce, and Energy. In fact, the only Cabinet Department that hasn't had a native New Yorker heading it is the Department of Transportation. New York is only the third most popular birth state of Presidents, birthing four of the 43.

2. PENNSYLVANIA saw the births of 53 Secretaries (and only one President). Twelve of the 82 Attorneys General were born in Pennsylvania, but its 53 Secretaries led only 14 of the 19 Cabinet Departments. No Pennsylvanians have been the Secretaries of Commerce & Labor, HEW, Education, Energy, or Veterans Affairs.

3. MASSACHUSETTS is the birth state of 53 Secretaries (and four Presidents), including the first two Secretaries of War. No one from Massachusetts has

led the Departments of Justice, Commerce & Labor, HHS, Education, Veterans Affairs, or Homeland Security.

4. VIRGINIA. The most popular state for Presidents to be born in (eight of the 43), it is the fourth most popular for Cabinet Secretaries (44). The first Secretary of State, Attorney General, and Secretary of the Interior were all born in Virginia. Third, fourth, and fifth Presidents Thomas Jefferson, James Madison, and James Monroe were all Virginians and were the first, fifth, and seventh Secretaries of State.

5. OHIO fathered 31 Secretaries and seven Presidents (second on that list). The first Ohioan to serve in the Cabinet was Edwin McMasters Stanton, who became the 25th Attorney General in December 1860.

At the other end of the spectrum, three states still have produced no Cabinet Secretaries: ALASKA, MONTANA, and NEVADA.

Six other states birthed one Secretary each: Hawaii, New Mexico, Rhode Island, South Dakota, Washington, and Wyoming:

HAWAII: seventh Secretary of Veterans Affairs Eric Shinseki (2009–14)
NEW MEXICO: 46th Secretary of the Interior Manuel Lujan, Jr. (1989–93)
RHODE ISLAND: 60th Attorney General J. Howard McGrath (1949–52)
SOUTH DAKOTA: 13th Secretary of Agriculture Clinton P. Anderson (1945–48)
WASHINGTON: 36th Secretary of Commerce Gary Locke (2009–11)
WYOMING: 43rd Secretary of the Interior James G. Watt (1981–83)

64. Foreign-Born Cabinet Secretaries

Twenty-six of the more than 600 Cabinet Secretaries were born in foreign countries, and that's not counting 51st Secretary of War Patrick Jay Hurley (1929–33), who was born in the Choctaw Nation (which would become Oklahoma) in 1883. The most popular foreign country is Germany, in which four future US Cabinet Secretaries were born. Scotland bore three, and Canada, France, Ireland, and Switzerland were the birth countries of two Secretaries each. The foreign-born Secretaries include three of the 68 Secretaries of State; seven of the 76 Secretaries of the Treasury (including four of the first six); four of the 51 Secretaries of the Interior; and three of the 26 Secretaries of Labor.

First Secretary of the Treasury ALEXANDER HAMILTON (1789–95) was born in Nevis, in the West Indies, on January 11, in either the year 1755 or 1757. He was killed in a duel with Vice President Aaron Burr on July 12, 1804, and buried in New York.

Third Secretary of War JAMES MCHENRY (1796–1800) was born in Ireland on November 16, 1753. He died in Maryland on May 3, 1816.

Fourth Secretary of the Treasury ALBERT GALLATIN (1801–14) was born in Switzerland on January 29, 1761. He died in New York on August 12, 1849.

Fifth Secretary of the Treasury GEORGE WASHINGTON CAMPBELL (February–October 1814) was born in Scotland on February 9, 1769. He died in Tennessee on February 17, 1848.

Sixth Secretary of the Treasury ALEXANDER JAMES DALLAS (1814–16) was born in Jamaica on June 21, 1759. He was the father of 11th Vice President

George Mifflin Dallas (1845–49). Secretary Dallas died in Pennsylvania on January 16, 1817.

Eleventh Secretary of the Treasury WILLIAM JOHN DUANE (May-September 1833) was born in Ireland on May 9, 1780. He died on September 27, 1865.

Fourteenth Attorney General HENRY D. GILPIN (1840–41) was born in England to US parents on April 14, 1801. He died January 29, 1860.

Tenth Secretary of the Interior JACOB DOLSON COX (1869–70) was born in Canada to US parents on October 27, 1828. He died in Ohio on August 4, 1900.

Thirteenth Secretary of the Interior CARL SCHURZ (1877–81) was born in Germany on March 2, 1829. He died in New York on May 14, 1906.

Fourth Secretary of Agriculture JAMES WILSON (1897–1913) was born in Scotland on August 16, 1835. His 16-year tenure makes him the longest-serving Cabinet Secretary in US history. He died in Iowa on August 26, 1920.

Third Secretary of Commerce & Labor OSCAR S. STRAUS (1906–09) was born in Germany on December 23, 1850. He also served as US Ambassador to the Ottoman Empire three separate times (1887–89, 1898–99, and 1909–10) and died in New York on May 3, 1926.

Twenty-sixth Secretary of the Interior FRANKLIN KNIGHT LANE (1913–20) was born in Canada on July 15, 1864. He died on May 18, 1921.

First Secretary of Labor WILLIAM B. WILSON (1913–21) was born in Scotland on April 2, 1862. He died in Pennsylvania on May 25, 1934.

Second Secretary of Labor JAMES J. DAVIS (1921–30) was born in Wales on October 27, 1873. He died in Pennsylvania on November 22, 1947.

Fifty-eighth Attorney General FRANCIS BIDDLE (1941–45) was born in France to US parents on May 9, 1886. He was the great-great-grandson of first Attorney General Edmund Randolph (who was also the second Secretary of State). Biddle died in Massachusetts on October 4, 1968.

Fifty-third Secretary of State CHRISTIAN ARCHIBALD HERTER (1959–61) was born in France on March 28, 1895. He died in Massachusetts on December 30, 1966.

Fifty-seventh Secretary of the Treasury CLARENCE DOUGLAS DILLON (1961–65) was born in Switzerland to US parents on August 21, 1909. He also served as Ambassador to France (1953–57) and died in New York on January 10, 2003.

Fifth Secretary of Health, Education, and Welfare ANTHONY J. CELEBREZZE (1962–65) was born in Italy on September 4, 1910. He died in Ohio on October 29, 1998.

Third Secretary of Housing and Urban Development GEORGE W. ROMNEY (1969–73) was born in Mexico on July 8, 1907, to American parents living in a Mormon colony (though they fled back to the United States when he was young, during the Mexican Revolution). He was the 43rd Governor of Michigan (1963–69), and his son, Mitt, was the Republican nominee for President in 2012. George died in Michigan on July 26, 1995.

Fifty-sixth Secretary of State HENRY KISSINGER (1973–77) was born in Germany on May 27, 1923. Before his Cabinet post, he was National Security Advisor and the co-winner of the 1973 Nobel Peace Prize with North Vietnamese representative Le Duc Tho.

Sixty-fourth Secretary of the Treasury W. MICHAEL BLUMENTHAL was born in Germany on January 3, 1926.

Sixty-fourth Secretary of State MADELEINE ALBRIGHT (1997–2001) was born in Czechoslovakia on May 15, 1937. She was the first female Secretary of State.

Twelfth Secretary of Housing and Urban Development MEL MARTINEZ (2001–03) was born in Cuba on October 23, 1946. In 1962, he came to the United States as part of a Roman Catholic humanitarian effort called Operation Peter Pan. He resigned from the Cabinet to run for the Senate and represented Florida in the Senate from 2005 to 2009, when he resigned to become a lobbyist and then a bank chairman.

Twenty-fourth Secretary of Labor ELAINE CHAO (2001–09) was born in Taiwan on March 26, 1953. She is married to Senator Mitch McConnell of Kentucky.

Thirty-fifth Secretary of Commerce CARLOS GUTIERREZ (2005–09) was born in Cuba on November 4, 1953.

Fifty-first Secretary of the Interior SALLY JEWELL (2013–) was born in England on February 21, 1956.

65. The Five Cabinet Secretaries Who Served the Longest Terms

Cabinet Secretaries are appointed by the President (with the advice and consent of the Senate), but have no Constitutional term limit, so one might assume the longest-serving Secretaries served during Franklin Roosevelt's 12-year term. But there's no legal bar to them serving more than one President (like Vice Presidents Clinton and Calhoun).

1. JAMES WILSON. The fourth Secretary of Agriculture was born in Scotland. He was appointed by Republican President William McKinley and took office on March 6, 1897. Following McKinley's assassination, Theodore Roosevelt kept him in the Cabinet, and through Roosevelt's own election. Roosevelt's hand-picked successor, William Howard Taft, also kept Wilson in the post. He left the Cabinet on March 5, 1913, when Democrat Woodrow Wilson took office. Secretary Wilson served 15 years, 364 days.

2. HAROLD L. ICKES. The 32nd Secretary of the Interior was appointed by Franklin Roosevelt when he took office, on March 4, 1933. He stayed on for all of Roosevelt's term and only left the Cabinet on February 15, 1946, after Harry Truman had been President for nearly a year. Ickes served 12 years, 348 days.

3. ALBERT GALLATIN. The fourth Secretary of the Treasury was born in Switzerland, the second in his post to have been born in a foreign country. He was appointed by Thomas Jefferson on May 14, 1801 (John Adams appointed Samuel Dexter toward the end of his term, and he stayed on for the first two months of Jefferson's). Gallatin held his post through Jefferson's reelection, as well as James Madison's two elections. He retired from the Treasury on February 8, 1814, having served 12 years, 268 days.

4. FRANCES PERKINS. The fourth Secretary of Labor was the first woman to serve in a Presidential Cabinet. She came to office with Franklin Roosevelt, taking the post on March 4, 1933. She served his entire term, resigning two months after Roosevelt's death, on June 30, 1945, having served 12 years, 118 days. She was the only woman to serve more than eight years in one Cabinet position.

5. CORDELL HULL. The 47th Secretary of State was another of Franklin Roosevelt's long-serving appointees. He took the job on March 4, 1933, and resigned November 30, 1944. He won the Nobel Peace Prize in 1945, for his efforts as Secretary of State.

Six other Secretaries served in one post for more than eight years:

Fifty-second Secretary of the Treasury HENRY MORGENTHAU, JR. Appointed by Franklin Roosevelt, he served January 1, 1934–July 22, 1945: 11 years, 172 days. His son, Robert Morgenthau, served as District Attorney of New York County, New York, from 1975 to 2009.

Ninth Attorney General WILLIAM WIRT. Appointed by James Monroe and John Quincy Adams, he served November 13, 1817–March 4, 1829: 11 years, 111 days.

Forty-ninth Secretary of the Treasury ANDREW WILLIAM MELLON. Appointed by Warren Harding, he served Harding, Calvin Coolidge, and Herbert Hoover from March 4, 1921, to February 12, 1932: 10 years, 345 days.

Second Secretary of Labor JAMES J. DAVIS. Born in Wales, he was appointed by Warren Harding and also served Calvin Coolidge and Herbert Hoover from March 5, 1921, to November 30, 1930: nine years, 270 days.

Seventh Secretary of the Treasury WILLIAM HARRIS CRAWFORD. Appointed by James Madison at the end of his term, he served from October 22, 1816, to March 6, 1825, mostly under James Monroe, for eight years, 135 days.

Twenty-second Secretary of the Interior ETHAN ALLEN HITCHCOCK. Appointed by William McKinley and kept on by Theodore Roosevelt, he served from February 20, 1899, to March 4, 1907: eight years, 12 days.

66. The Five Cabinet Secretaries Who Served the Shortest Terms

The shortest Presidential term of office was William Henry Harrison's 31 days. The shortest Vice Presidential term (other than those who succeeded to the Presidency) was William R.D. King's 45 days. But six Cabinet secretaries served terms of less than one month.

1. THOMAS WALKER GILMER. The 15th Secretary of the Navy served a scant nine days in his post, from February 19 to 28, 1844. The 41-year-old Virginian was one of those killed in the explosion aboard the USS *Princeton*.

2. THOMAS McKEAN THOMPSON McKENNAN. The second Secretary of the Interior served 11 days, from August 15 to 26, 1850. He represented Pennsylvania in the House of Representatives from 1831 to 1839, again in 1842 and 1843, and then refused to run again, saying he'd done his duty by serving in public office. He was reluctant to accept the Cabinet position Millard Fillmore offered him, but acquiesced to the pressure of friends and associates urging him to accept. He instantly regretted his decision and resigned. He died in July of 1852, aged 58.

3. ELIHU B. WASHBURNE. The 25th Secretary of State served 12 days. He took office with President Grant, on March 5, 1869, and left the post on the 16th of the month. He then served eight years as Ambassador to France. His successor as Secretary, Hamilton Fish, stayed until the end of Grant's Presidency.

4. ROBERT C. WOOD. The second Secretary of Housing and Urban Development was the department's first Under Secretary and then Acting Secretary from his predecessor Robert C. Weaver's retirement on December

18, 1968. Wood was confirmed in his own right and served as Secretary from January 7, 1969, and served until the end of Lyndon Johnson's term of office, on the 20th. After his government service, he returned to academia at MIT, Harvard, and the University of Massachusetts.

5. NORMAN JAY COLEMAN. The first Secretary of Agriculture was appointed by Grover Cleveland at the end of his first term, when the post was created. He served from February 15 to March 6, 1889, but was not confirmed by the Senate.

6. HORATIO KING. The 19th Postmaster General was appointed by James Buchanan at the end of his term and served 25 days, from February 12 to March 7, 1861. The 49-year-old from Maine then lived another 36 years as a retired Cabinet Secretary.

7. JOSEPH WALKER BARR. The 59th Secretary of the Treasury served 30 days. He was appointed by Lyndon Johnson at the end of his term and served from December 21, 1968, until Richard Nixon took office on January 20, 1969.

And no fewer than 103 Secretaries served terms less than one year long.

67. The Five Cabinet Secretaries Who Served the Most Presidents

Cabinet Secretaries have no term limits, and there's no Constitutional bar to them remaining in office in perpetuity, as long as Presidents keep appointing them. Of the more than 600 Cabinet Secretaries approved by the Senate, one has served under four Presidents, and 12 others have served under three.

1. HENRY L. STIMSON was born in New York in 1867. On May 22, 1911, William Howard Taft appointed Stimson the 45th Secretary of War (Taft himself had been the 42nd). He stayed in office until the end of Taft's term. On March 28, 1929, Herbert Hoover made Stimson the 46th Secretary of State, and they both left office on March 4, 1933, when Franklin Roosevelt became President. On July 10, 1940, however, Roosevelt returned Stimson to his post at the War Department, this time as the 54th Secretary. He resigned this time on September 21, 1945 (his 78th birthday), five months after Harry Truman took office. He died in 1950.

In chronological order, the Secretaries who served under three Presidents were:

RICHARD RUSH was born in Pennsylvania in 1780. James Madison appointed him the eighth Attorney General on February 10, 1814, and James Monroe kept him for his first year. Rush resigned the post on November 12, 1817. Upon taking office in 1825, John Quincy Adams appointed Rush the eighth Secretary of the Treasury, and Rush served Adams's entire term. He died in 1859.

JOHN C. CALHOUN was born in South Carolina in 1782. Following William Harris Crawford's elevation to Secretary of State, James Monroe appointed

Calhoun the 10th Secretary of War on October 8, 1817, and Calhoun served the remainder of Monroe's term. While serving as Secretary of War, Calhoun was elected Vice President under John Quincy Adams. In 1828, he became the second Vice President to be elected with two different Presidents, continuing in the office under Andrew Jackson. He resigned the Vice Presidency in December 1832 to take his seat in the Senate, representing his home state. Toward the end of his term, John Tyler called Calhoun out of retirement to serve as the 16th Secretary of State. Calhoun held that post from April 1, 1844, until March 10, 1845, serving also, for a few days, under James Polk. He died in 1850, while serving a second time in the Senate.

JOHN J. CRITTENDEN was born in Kentucky in 1786. In 1841, William Henry Harrison appointed him the 15th Attorney General. Harrison died after one month in office, and John Tyler succeeded. Crittenden resigned his office on September 12, 1841, serving only 191 days total under two Presidents. Soon after assuming the Presidency, Millard Fillmore appointed Crittenden the 22nd Attorney General, on July 22, 1850. This time, Crittenden served until the end of Fillmore's term. He died in 1863.

EDWIN MCMASTERS STANTON was born in Ohio in 1814. At the end of his term, James Buchanan appointed Stanton the 25th Attorney General, and he served 74 days, from December 20, 1860, to March 4, 1861. On January 20, 1862, Abraham Lincoln appointed Stanton Secretary of War. After Lincoln's death, he served under Andrew Johnson, but it was his machinations against the President that made Johnson attempt to fire him, despite the Tenure of Office Act, in February 1868. Stanton refused to leave and barricaded himself in the War Department. Johnson was impeached, but ultimately acquitted in May 1868, and Stanton left office on May 28, 1868. He died the following year.

HUGH MCCULLOCH was born in Maine in 1808. At the start of his second term, Abraham Lincoln appointed McCulloch the 27th Secretary of the Treasury. Following his assassination a month later, Andrew Johnson kept

McCulloch for his entire term. On October 31, 1884, Chester Arthur chose McCulloch to be his third Secretary of the Treasury (and the nation's 36th). McCulloch served out the remainder of Arthur's term, 127 days. He died in 1895.

JAMES G. BLAINE was born in Pennsylvania in 1830. James Garfield appointed him the 28th Secretary of State on March 7, 1881. After Garfield's death, Blaine served under Chester Arthur only a few more months, resigning on December 19, 1881. When Benjamin Harrison took office in 1889, he again appointed Blaine to the State Department, this time as the 31st Secretary. Blaine resigned the post on June 4, 1892. He died in 1893. His grandnephew, James Blaine Walker, married Harrison's daughter Elizabeth in 1922.

JAMES WILSON was born in Scotland in 1835. After immigrating to the United States, he settled in Iowa, but spent a long time in Washington. William McKinley appointed him the fourth Secretary of Agriculture when he took office, on March 6, 1897, and Wilson kept the post for all of Theodore Roosevelt's and William Howard Taft's terms. He left office on March 5, 1913, one day before his 16th anniversary on the job. He was the longest-serving Cabinet Secretary, and he died in 1920.

PHILANDER C. KNOX. He was born in 1853; William McKinley appointed him the 45th Attorney General on April 5, 1901. He stayed on in that post under Theodore Roosevelt and resigned on June 30, 1904, to take his seat in the Senate representing Pennsylvania. On March 6, 1909, William Howard Taft appointed Knox the 40th Secretary of State, and he held that post for Taft's entire term. He died in 1921.

JAMES J. DAVIS was born in Wales in 1873. After immigrating to the United States, he settled in Pennsylvania. Warren Harding appointed him the second Secretary of Labor when he took office, and Calvin Coolidge and Herbert Hoover kept him on the job. He retired on November 30, 1930. He died in 1947.

ANDREW WILLIAM MELLON was born in Pennsylvania in 1855. When he took office, Warren Harding appointed Mellon the 49th Secretary of the Treasury. Calvin Coolidge kept him on when he succeeded to the Presidency. And when Hebert Hoover was elected President, he, too, kept Mellon on the job. Mellon resigned on February 12, 1932, and Hoover appointed him Ambassador to the United Kingdom. He died in 1937.

JAMES R. SCHLESINGER was born in New York in 1929. On July 2, 1973, Richard Nixon appointed him his third Secretary of Defense (and 12th overall). Schlesinger was also the third Secretary of Defense that year, after serving the first seven months of the year as Director of Central Intelligence. After Nixon's resignation, Schlesinger stayed on in the Ford Administration. He resigned on November 19, 1975. On August 6, 1977, Jimmy Carter appointed Schlesinger the first Secretary of Energy. He resigned that post on August 6, 1979, and died in 2014.

CASPER W. WEINBERGER was born in California in 1917. Richard Nixon appointed him the 10th Secretary of Health, Education, and Welfare on February 12, 1973. Nixon resigned in August 1974, and Gerald Ford took office. Weinberger resigned on August 8, 1975. When Ronald Reagan took office in 1981, he appointed Weinberger the 15th Secretary of Defense. Weinberger resigned that position on November 23, 1987. He died in 2006.

68. The Five Cabinet Secretaries Who Served in the Greatest Number of Different Posts

Of the more than 600 Cabinet Secretaries appointed, 41 people have served as the heads of more than one department.

ELLIOT L. RICHARDSON is the only person to serve as the head of four separate departments. On June 24, 1970, Richard Nixon appointed the 50-year-old lawyer from Massachusetts the ninth Secretary of Health, Education, and Welfare. On January 30, 1973, Nixon moved him to a different post, making him the 11th Secretary of Defense. Richardson kept his office in the Pentagon a scant 114 days, before Nixon moved him over to be the 69th Attorney General. He served in that job only 148 days, resigning October 20, 1973. In 1975, Gerald Ford appointed him Ambassador to the United Kingdom. And then, on February 2, 1976, Ford called him back home to take up his post as the 23rd Secretary of Commerce. This time, he was in office for 352 days, leaving when Ford left office, on January 20, 1977. Richardson died December 31, 1999.

Three others served as the head of three different departments each:

WALTER Q. GRESHAM. On April 3, 1883, Chester Arthur appointed the 51-year-old Indianan the 31st Postmaster General. On September 5, 1884, Arthur moved Gresham over to be the 35th Secretary of the Treasury. Gresham resigned that position 55 days later, on October 30, 1884. When Grover Cleveland took office for the second time, he appointed Gresham the 33rd Secretary of State. Gresham served from March 7, 1893, until he died in office on May 28, 1895.

GEORGE B. CORTELYOU. In 1903, the Department of Commerce and Labor was formed under Theodore Roosevelt, and on February 18 of that year, the

40-year-old from New York became its first Secretary. Cortelyou resigned on June 30, 1904. Roosevelt called him back to the Cabinet, appointing him the 42nd Postmaster General on March 6, 1905. He left that office on January 14, 1907, but on March 4 of the same year (still under Roosevelt), he took over as the 44th Secretary of the Treasury. This time, he stayed until the end of the term and left the Treasury on March 7, 1909, days after William Howard Taft took office. Cortelyou died in 1940.

GEORGE P. SHULTZ. On January 22, 1969, at the age of 48, Shultz became the 11th Secretary of Labor. He resigned on July 1, 1970. On June 12, 1972, Nixon appointed him the 62nd Secretary of the Treasury. He resigned on May 8, 1974, three months before Nixon himself resigned. On July 16, 1982, after a year and a half in office, Ronald Reagan appointed Shultz the 60th Secretary of State. He served until the end of Reagan's term.

Two other men served as the heads of only two departments, but held one of the posts twice:

JOHN Y. MASON. A month before his 45th birthday, Mason was appointed the 16th Secretary of the Navy by John Tyler. He served from March 26, 1844, until Tyler left office on March 4, 1845. Mason, however, didn't leave the Cabinet: incoming President James Polk appointed him the 18th Attorney General, where he served from March 5, 1845, to October 16, 1846 (until Nathan Clifford was confirmed to succeed him). On September 10, 1846, after Mason's successor as Secretary of the Navy, George Bancroft, was appointed Ambassador to England, Mason returned as the 18th Secretary of the Navy. He stayed in this post until the end of Polk's term, on March 4, 1849. Mason was later Ambassador to France, from 1853 until his death in office in October 1859.

HENRY L. STIMSON is the only Cabinet Secretary to serve under four Presidents. On May 22, 1911, William Howard Taft appointed him the 45th Secretary of War. He stayed in office until the end of Taft's term. On March 28, 1929, Herbert Hoover made Stimson the 46th Secretary of

State, and they both left office on March 4, 1933, when Franklin Roosevelt became President. On July 10, 1940, however, Roosevelt returned Stimson to his post at the War Department, this time as the 54th Secretary. He resigned this time on September 21, 1945 (his 78th birthday), five months after Harry Truman took office. He died in 1950.

Four other people have served non-consecutive terms in single Cabinet posts:

JOHN J. CRITTENDEN was the 15th Attorney General (March 5–September 12, 1841, under William Henry Harrison and John Tyler) and the 22nd Attorney General (July 22, 1850–March 4, 1853, under Millard Fillmore).

HUGH MCCULLOCH was the 27th Secretary of the Treasury (March 9, 1865–March 3, 1869, under Abraham Lincoln and Andrew Johnson) and the 36th Secretary of the Treasury (October 31, 1884–March 7, 1885, under Chester Arthur).

JAMES G. BLAINE was the 28th Secretary of State (March 7–December 28, 1881, under James Garfield and Chester Arthur) and the 31st Secretary of State (March 7, 1889–June 4, 1892, under Benjamin Harrison).

DONALD RUMSFELD was 43 years old (the youngest to hold the office) when he was appointed the 13th Secretary of Defense (November 20, 1975–January 20, 1977, under Gerald Ford). Later, at the age of 68 (the oldest appointed to the job—until 73-year-old Leon Panetta took office in 2011), he became the 21st Secretary of Defense (January 20, 2001–December 18, 2006, under George W. Bush).

69. The Cabinet Secretaries Who Later Became President

1. THOMAS JEFFERSON was the first Secretary of State, serving from 1790 to 1793. He organized the department, but clashed frequently with Secretary of the Treasury Alexander Hamilton. Jefferson resigned when it became clear to him that President Washington was favoring Hamilton's views. In 1796, he was elected the second Vice President, under John Adams, and defeated Adams in the election of 1800 to become the third President.

2. JAMES MADISON was the fifth Secretary of State, serving under Thomas Jefferson for his entire eight-year term (1801–09). Madison supported the Louisiana Purchase, encouraged resistance to the tribute the Barbary Pirates demanded, and urged an embargo against Britain and France in retaliation for their harassment of US ships (and especially for British impressment of US sailors). Madison was Jefferson's chosen successor for the Presidency and was elected in 1808 and again in 1812.

3. JAMES MONROE was the seventh Secretary of State (April 2, 1811–March 9, 1817). He could not find a peaceful solution to the problems with Great Britain and concluded that war could not be more injurious than the tense state of relations between the nations. He ordered the evacuation of all important papers from the State Department in advance of the British invasion of Washington in 1814. After the British withdrawal, James Madison appointed Monroe the eighth Secretary of War (September 27, 1814–March 12, 1815) and military commander of the Federal District (concurrent with his duties as Secretary of State). Though he was unable to convince Congress of the need for a draft, he was able to strengthen the Army by offering greater inducements for service. He was Madison's heir apparent and won the Presidency in 1816, and again in 1820.

4. JOHN QUINCY ADAMS was the eighth Secretary of State for all eight years of James Monroe's Presidency (1817–25). He negotiated the Convention of 1818 with Britain, establishing the US-Canadian border from Minnesota to the Rocky Mountains. He concluded the Adams-Onís Treaty with Spain in 1819, transferring Spanish Florida to the United States, fixing the southern boundary of the United States, and removing Spanish claims to Oregon. And he was instrumental in the form and content of the Monroe Doctrine. He then won the four-way free-for-all that was the election of 1824, which was decided by the House of Representatives.

5. MARTIN VAN BUREN was the 10th Secretary of State, serving under Andrew Jackson from March 28, 1829, to May 23, 1831. He negotiated a commercial treaty with Turkey in 1830, gaining navigation rights on the Black Sea for the United States. Also in 1830, he negotiated a treaty with Great Britain, renewing US rights to trade with the West Indies. And he helped win reparations from France for losses incurred during the Napoleonic Wars. He resigned in 1831 to help Jackson with an overall Cabinet shake-up. Jackson named Van Buren minister to Great Britain, but the Senate rejected the nomination. In 1832, Van Buren was elected Jackson's second Vice President (John C. Calhoun was dropped from the ticket), and in 1836, Van Buren won his own term as President.

6. JAMES BUCHANAN was the 17th Secretary of State, under James Knox Polk, from March 10, 1845, to March 7, 1849. Polk directed most foreign policy himself, limiting Buchanan's influence. He did make the final arrangements for the annexation of Texas and negotiated the 1846 Oregon Treaty with Great Britain, fixing the US-Canadian border in the far west at the 49th parallel (giving present-day Washington and Oregon to the United States and all of Vancouver Island to Canada). He had previously served in the House and the Senate, and as US Minister to Russia. From 1853 to 1856, he was US Minister to Great Britain, and then he was elected President in 1856.

7. WILLIAM HOWARD TAFT was the 42nd Secretary of War, serving under Theodore Roosevelt from February 1, 1904, to June 30, 1908, when he

resigned in order to run for President (he served one term, from 1909 to 1913). He supervised preparations for the construction of the Panama Canal and personally inspected the site in November and December 1904. In July 1905, he met with Japanese Premier Count Taro Katsura and assured Katsura that the United States would not oppose the Japanese taking over Korea, as long as it was not a prelude to aggression against the Philippines; Roosevelt approved the deal after the fact. Taft was in the Philippines from July to September 1905. He was the provisional Governor of Cuba during September–October 1906. Taft also served as Acting Secretary of State during John Hay's final illness (he died in office in 1905). Taft's father, Alphonso, was the 31st Secretary of War, serving under Ulysses Grant from March 8 to May 22, 1876 (he was then the 34th Attorney General, from May 22, 1876, to March 4, 1877).

8. HERBERT HOOVER was the third Secretary of Commerce, serving under Warren Harding and Calvin Coolidge from March 5, 1921, to August 21, 1928. Hoover was very active in his post, expanding the Bureau of Standards and the amount of data collected by the Census Bureau. He established the Aeronautics Board under the Air Commerce Act of 1926, started the regulation of the airwaves under the Radio Act of 1927, worked to increase food exports and improve the nation's inland waterways, and persuaded the steel industry to abandon the 12-hour workday. He pushed for the construction of the St. Lawrence Seaway and the Boulder Dam (which was later renamed in his honor). He was a candidate for the Vice Presidential nomination in 1924, but lost out to Charles G. Dawes. He resigned from the Cabinet when he won the Republican nomination for President in 1928, and served one term in the Presidency.

And the two "almosts":

THEODORE ROOSEVELT was Assistant Secretary of the Navy from 1897 to 1898. He advocated expansion and war with Spain, and served as Acting Secretary during the prolonged absences of ailing Secretary John D. Long. He resigned to volunteer to serve in the Spanish-American War. In 1900, he was elected Vice President and succeeded to the Presidency upon William McKinley's death. He then became the first President to succeed to the office and then win election to his own term, in 1904.

FRANKLIN DELANO ROOSEVELT was Assistant Secretary of the Navy from 1913 to 1920. He proposed expansion of the Navy, drew up war contingency plans as early as 1913, and was an early advocate of US entry into World War I. During the war, he directed the mining of waters between Scotland and Norway. He also took two inspection tours of naval bases and war zones in Europe, July–September 1918 and January–February 1919. He resigned in 1920 to accept the Democratic nomination for Vice President under James M. Cox. He lost that election, but was elected President in 1932, 1936, 1940, and 1944.

70. The Presidents Who Had the Greatest Number of People Serve in Their Cabinets

This list is naturally skewed toward the more recent Presidents, because the size of the Cabinet has changed over time, from the four officers who served George Washington (Secretaries of State, Treasury, and War, and Attorney General) to the 15 who served Barack Obama.

1. HARRY S TRUMAN (34 Cabinet officers, an average of 3.4 per department). Truman started his Presidency with 10 Cabinet positions, but the Departments of War and the Navy were combined into the Department of Defense during his term (in 1947). The last Secretary of the Navy, James V. Forrestal, became the first Secretary of Defense. Three members of Truman's Cabinet (all holdovers from Franklin Roosevelt's Cabinet) are among the longest-serving Cabinet Secretaries: Secretary of the Interior Harold L. Ickes, who served from 1933 to 1946; Secretary of Labor Frances Perkins (the first woman to serve in the Cabinet), who served from 1933 to 1945; and Secretary of the Treasury Henry Morgenthau, Jr., who served from 1934 to 1945.

2. RONALD REAGAN (33 Cabinet officers, an average of 2.5 per department). Reagan had 13 separate Cabinet departments, eight of which had three Secretaries each. The only Cabinet member to serve all eight years of the Reagan Administration was Secretary of Housing and Urban Development Samuel R. Pierce, Jr.

3 (tie). RICHARD NIXON (31 Cabinet officers, an average of 2.6 per department). Nixon had 12 Cabinet departments and had four Secretaries of the Treasury and four Attorneys General. The only Cabinet member to not

be replaced was Postmaster General Winton Blount, who supervised the conversion of his department into the independent government agency now known as the US Postal Service and thus removed himself from the Cabinet.

3 (tie). GEORGE W. BUSH (31 Cabinet officers, an average of 2.2 per department). Bush had 14 Cabinet departments (including Homeland Security, which was created during his Administration). Only one Cabinet Secretary served his entire eight-year term: Secretary of Labor Elaine Chao, who was the first Chinese American and first Asian American woman in the Cabinet. Donald Rumsfeld, Bush's first Secretary of Defense, was the oldest person appointed to that post (at the age of 68). During Gerald Ford's Administration, Rumsfeld had been the youngest Secretary of Defense (appointed at the age of 43).

5 (tie). THEODORE ROOSEVELT (29 Cabinet officers, an average of 3.2 per department). In only nine Cabinet departments, and seven and a half years in office, Roosevelt went through more Cabinet officers than any President before him. His six Secretaries of the Navy (John D. Long, William H. Moody, Paul Morton, Charles J. Bonaparte, Victor H. Metcalf, and Truman H. Newberry) were the most any President had in any one Cabinet post. At the other extreme, Secretary of Agriculture James Wilson was the longest-serving Cabinet official in US history (he served in that post from 1897 to 1913, and was the only Secretary of Agriculture for Presidents McKinley, Roosevelt, and Taft).

5 (tie). BILL CLINTON (29 Cabinet officers, an average of 2.1 per department). Four of Clinton's Cabinet officers served out his entire eight-year term: Attorney General Janet Reno (the first woman to hold the post), Secretary of the Interior Bruce Babbitt, Secretary of Health and Human Services Donna Shalala, and Secretary of Education Richard W. Riley.

If we take the measure as being the greatest number of officers per Cabinet department, it's better to split the list into the Presidents serving two terms and those serving one. Of the Presidents serving two terms:

1. ULYSSES GRANT averaged 3.6 officers per department (25 Secretaries, seven departments). No Secretary served the entire eight years. Grant had five Secretaries of War and five Attorneys General. Alphonso Taft was Grant's fourth Secretary of War, his fifth Attorney General, and the father of President William Howard Taft.

2 (tie). JAMES MADISON averaged 3.2 officers per department (16 Secretaries, five departments), including his second Secretary of State, James Monroe, who succeeded him as President, and the long-serving Secretary of the Treasury Albert Gallatin (1801–14).

2 (tie). ANDREW JACKSON averaged 3.2 officers per department (19 Secretaries, six departments), including his first Secretary of State, Martin Van Buren (who was later his Vice President and then succeeded him as President) and five Secretaries of the Treasury.

2 (tie). THEODORE ROOSEVELT averaged 3.2 officers per department (29 Secretaries, nine departments, see above).

2 (tie). HARRY TRUMAN averaged 3.2 officers per department (34 Secretaries, 10 departments, see above).

Of the Presidents serving only one term:

1. JOHN TYLER averaged 3.5 officers per department (21 Secretaries, six departments). Tyler succeeded to the Presidency after one month as Vice President, inheriting William Henry Harrison's short-serving officers. Tyler broke with his Whig Party in September 1841, prompting the entire Cabinet (except Secretary of State Daniel Webster) to resign.

2. CHESTER ARTHUR averaged 2.4 officers per department (17 Secretaries, seven departments). Arthur inherited James Garfield's Cabinet when Garfield died six months into his term. Five of the seven resigned or asked to be replaced, rather than serve Arthur. Secretary of War Robert Todd Lincoln (former President Abraham Lincoln's son) was the only Garfield appointee to serve Arthur's entire term.

3. GERALD FORD averaged 2.1 officers per department (23 Secretaries, 11 departments) during his two and a half years in office. Ford's second Secretary of Defense, Donald Rumsfeld, was the youngest man ever to hold that post (President George W. Bush also made him the oldest in the position in 2001). His third Secretary of Commerce, Elliot L. Richardson, was the only man to hold four separate Cabinet positions (he was Richard Nixon's Secretary of Health, Education, and Welfare; Secretary of Defense; and Attorney General).

4. JAMES BUCHANAN averaged 2.0 officers per department (14 Secretaries, seven departments). He is the first on this list to have served a complete four-year term.

5. ANDREW JOHNSON averaged 1.9 officers per department (13 Secretaries, seven departments). He inherited Abraham Lincoln's Cabinet. When Johnson discovered Secretary of War Edwin Stanton was working against his policies, Johnson fired Stanton in contravention of the Tenure of Office Act. The firing precipitated Johnson's impeachment.

Only four Presidents served their terms without replacing any Cabinet officers:

1. WILLIAM HENRY HARRISON. He was President for only one month, until he died in office. He actually didn't have time to do much of anything, let alone replace any of the six Cabinet officers.

2. ZACHARY TAYLOR. During his 16-month term, his original Cabinet stayed intact.

3. FRANKLIN PIERCE. Pierce is the only President to have served a full term with his original Cabinet. Secretary of State William Marcy died three months after leaving office. Secretary of War Jefferson Davis later served as President of the Confederate States of America.

4. JAMES ABRAM GARFIELD. Like Harrison before him, Garfield's incredibly short term (he was shot four months into his term and died two months later) prevented much action.

71. The Presidents Who Had the Greatest Number of People Serve in One Cabinet Post

1. THEODORE ROOSEVELT had six Secretaries of the Navy during his seven and a half years in office. John D. Long was a holdover from the McKinley Administration and had been Roosevelt's boss when he was Assistant Secretary of the Navy (1897–98); he resigned in 1902 to become a Senator. William H. Moody resigned from the House of Representatives and then transferred to Attorney General in 1904. Paul Morton served until 1905. Charles J. Bonaparte was a grandnephew of Napoleon, and he transferred to Attorney General in 1906. Victor H. Metcalf transferred from Secretary of Commerce and Labor, and resigned in 1908. Truman H. Newberry was a veteran naval officer and was promoted from Assistant Secretary of the Navy to finish out Roosevelt's term.

2 (tie). ANDREW JACKSON had five Secretaries of the Treasury during his eight-year term: Samuel D. Ingham; Louis McLane (who was transferred to Secretary of State in 1833); William J. Duane (who served four months in 1833); Roger B. Taney (who had been Attorney General and whom Jackson later appointed Chief Justice); and Levi Woodbury (who stayed on in the Van Buren Administration).

2 (tie). JOHN TYLER had five Secretaries of the Navy during his four years in office: George E. Badger (was part of the mass Cabinet resignation in September 1841); Abel P. Upshur (he resigned to become Secretary of State and was killed on February 28, 1844, in an explosion during an inspection of the warship USS *Princeton*); David Henshaw (who served only a few months); Thomas W. Gilmer (served February 19–28, 1844, he was killed in the same explosion the killed Upshur); and John Y. Mason

(who would become Polk's Attorney General and then his Secretary of the Navy).

2 (tie). ULYSSES GRANT had five Secretaries of War during his eight-year term: John A. Rawlins (served March–September 1869 and died in office of tuberculosis); William T. Sherman (served September–October 1869); William W. Belknap (served 1869–76; the House of Representatives voted to impeach him for accepting bribes, and he resigned); Alphonso Taft (served March–May 1876 and resigned to become Attorney General; his son William Howard was elected President in 1908); and James D. Cameron (he was the son of Abraham Lincoln's Secretary of War Simon Cameron).

2 (tie). ULYSSES GRANT had five Attorneys General: Ebenezer R. Hoar (served 1869–70; Grant nominated him to the Supreme Court, but the Senate refused to confirm him); Amos T. Akerman (served 1870–71; the railroads forced Grant to fire him); George H. Williams (served 1872–75; Grant nominated him to be Chief Justice, but he withdrew his nomination when it was revealed he'd suppressed an investigation into election fraud); Edwards Pierrepont (he resigned to become minister to Great Britain); and Alphonso Taft (see above).

2 (tie). THEODORE ROOSEVELT had five Postmasters General: Charles E. Smith (served 1898–1902, he was a holdover from the McKinley Administration); Henry C. Payne (died in office in 1904); Robert J. Wynne (served 1904–05); George B. Cortelyou (served 1905–07; one of only five men to serve in three Cabinet positions, he had been Roosevelt's Secretary of Commerce and Labor, and was later his Secretary of the Treasury); and George Meyer (he had been Ambassador to Italy and Russia, and served as Secretary of the Navy under President Taft).

PRESIDENTIAL SUCCESSION

The Vice President has only two Constitutional duties: to preside over the Senate and to be available to step into the Presidency if necessary.

Specifically, Article I, Section 3 says, "The Vice President of the United States shall be President of the Senate, but shall have no Vote, unless they be equally divided." And John Adams, as the first Vice President, jumped right into that role, while thinking very little of it. He wrote to his wife in December 1793, "My country has in its wisdom contrived for me the most insignificant office that ever the invention of man contrived or his imagination conceived."

Over the following two centuries, many of his successors and political pundits agreed with his opinion, and yet the institution of the Vice Presidency has been a major factor in the stability of the nation. The presence of a Vice President has provided a near-instantaneous replacement/continuation for the chief executive/figurehead of the United States each of the nine times the President has been unable to finish his elected term.

And that role, only invoked those nine times, has been the subject of far more thought and words. Article II, Section 1 of the Constitution originally said, "In Case of the Removal of the President from Office, or of his Death, Resignation, or Inability to discharge the Powers and Duties of the said Office, the Same shall devolve on the Vice President, and the Congress may by Law provide for the Case of Removal, Death, Resignation or

Inability, both of the President and Vice President, declaring what Officer shall then act as President, and such Officer shall act accordingly, until the Disability be removed, or a President shall be elected." Congress further defined that role several times: the untitled Presidential succession act of 1792 (approved March 1, 1792); the Presidential Succession Act of 1886 (approved January 19, 1886), which in part repealed the act of 1792; and Public Law 80–199, the Presidential Succession Act of 1947 (enacted July 18, 1947), which in part repealed the act of 1886. Finally, in 1967, Article II, Section 1 was superseded by the 25th Amendment.

All of that thinking, and the only times it has actually been put into practice have been following the eight Presidential deaths in office and one resignation, when those nine Vice Presidents succeeded to the Presidency. Further, following the adoption of the 25th Amendment, it has twice been employed to fill vacancies in the Vice Presidency. But in more than two and a quarter centuries, never have we had to look to any other officials to fill a multiple vacancy (though the possibility is frequently discussed in fiction).

72. The Presidential Succession
Act of 1792

The 1792 act was merely a few sections of a larger federal statute. It read:

Chap. VIII. — An Act relative to the Election of a President and Vice President of the United States, and declaring the Officer who shall act as President in case of Vacancies in the offices both of President and Vice President. . . .

Sec. 9. And be it further enacted, That in case of removal, death, resignation or inability both of the President and Vice President of the United States, the President of the Senate pro tempore, and in case there shall be no President of the Senate, then the Speaker of the House of Representatives, for the time being shall act as President of the United States until the disability be removed or a President shall be elected.

Sec. 10. And be it further enacted, That whenever the offices of President and Vice President shall both become vacant, the Secretary of State shall forthwith cause a notification thereof to be made to the executive of every state, and shall also cause the same to be published in at least one of the newspapers printed in each state, specifying that electors of the President of the United States shall be appointed or chosen in the several states within thirty-four days preceding the first Wednesday in December then next ensuing: Provided, There shall be the space of two months between the date of such notification and the said first Wednesday in December, but if there shall not be the space of two months between the date of such notification and the first Wednesday in December; and if the term for which the President and Vice President last in office were elected shall not expire on the third day of March next ensuing, then the Secretary of State shall specify in the notification that the electors shall be appointed or chosen within thirty-four days preceding the first Wednesday in December in the year next ensuing, within which time the electors shall accordingly be appointed or chosen, and the electors shall meet and give their votes on the said first Wednesday in December, and the proceedings and duties of the said electors and others shall be pursuant to the directions prescribed in this act.

Sec. 11. And be it further enacted, That the only evidence of a refusal to accept or of a resignation of the office of President or Vice President, shall be an instrument in writing declaring the same, and subscribed by the person refusing to accept or resigning, as the case may be, and delivered into the office of the Secretary of State.

Sec. 12. And be it further enacted, That the term of four years for which a President and Vice President shall be elected shall in all cases commence on the fourth day of March next succeeding the day on which the votes of the electors shall have been given.

This act set the President pro tempore of the Senate and then the Speaker of the House of Representatives as next in line for the Presidency after the Vice President, but went no further than those three. From its adoption in 1792 until it was superseded by the act of 1886, it was never employed. There were 10 instances when the Vice Presidency was vacant, meaning the President pro tempore was next in line to be Acting President:

Vice Presidents John Tyler (in 1841), Millard Fillmore (in 1850), Andrew Johnson (in 1865), and Chester Arthur (in 1881) succeeded to the Presidency following the deaths of their predecessors. Vice Presidents George Clinton (in 1812), Elbridge Gerry (in 1814), William King (in 1853), Henry Wilson (in 1875), and Thomas Hendricks (in 1885) died in office. And Vice President John Calhoun resigned in the waning months of 1832.

Several times in those 94 years, there was a real possibility of needing to fill a multiple vacancy:

On February 28, 1844, President John Tyler was aboard the USS *Princeton* when its cannon exploded, killing Secretary of State Abel P. Upshur, Secretary of the Navy Thomas Walker Gilmer, Tyler's future father-in-law David Gardiner, and three others. Tyler, fortunately, was below decks at the time and not injured, but had he died, President pro tempore Willie Person Mangum was next in line for the Presidency. Mangum was a 51-year-old Senator from North Carolina and President pro tempore from May 1842 to March 1845.

The night John Wilkes Booth assassinated President Abraham Lincoln, April 14, 1865, there was actually a much larger plot afoot. Two other accomplices intended to assassinate Vice President Andrew Johnson and Secretary of State William H. Seward. Seward's assassin, Lewis Powell, severely wounded Seward. Johnson's assassin, George Atzerodt, never acted. Had Johnson been killed, President pro tempore Lafayette S. Foster was next in line. The 58-year-old Senator from Connecticut was President pro tempore from March 1865 to March 1867.

In 1868, President Andrew Johnson was impeached by the House of Representatives. The Senate acquitted him by a scant one-vote margin. Had the Senate instead convicted, Johnson would have been removed from office, and 67-year-old Benjamin Wade of Ohio—President pro tempore from March 1867 to March 1869—would have taken over.

Additionally, when President James Garfield finally succumbed to his wounds on September 19, 1881 (he had been shot on July 2), and Vice President Chester Arthur took the oath of office as President (in the early hours of September 20), Arthur was at his home in New York City. With his accession to the Presidency, there was no Vice President. Congress was not in session (the 46th Congress had adjourned in March, and the 47th was not scheduled to convene until December), so there was no President pro tempore of the Senate and no Speaker of the House. Had Arthur died at that point, there would have been no clear successor. To avoid such a catastrophe, Arthur drafted a proclamation calling the Senate into special session and mailed it to the White House. When he arrived in Washington two days later, he was able to destroy the letter and call the Senate into session himself.

73. The Presidential Succession
Act of 1886

The Presidential Succession Act of 1886 reads:

Jan. 19, 1886.

    Chap. 4.—An act to provide for the performance of the duties of the office of President in case of the removal, death, resignation, or inability both of the President and Vice-President.

    PROVISION FOR ACTING PRESIDENT SHOULD VACANCY OCCUR IN BOTH OFFICES. *In case of removal, death, resignation, or inability of both the President and Vice-President of the United States, the Secretary of State, or if there be none, or in case of his removal, death, resignation, or inability, then the Secretary of the Treasury, or if there be none, or in case of his removal, death, resignation, or inability, then the Secretary of War, or if there be none, or in case of his removal, death, resignation, or inability, then the Attorney-General, or if there be none, or in case of his removal, death, resignation, or inability, then the Postmaster-General, or if there be none, or in case of his removal, death, resignation, or inability, then the Secretary of the Navy, or if there be none, or in case of his removal, death, resignation, or inability, then the Secretary of the Interior, shall act as President until the disability of the President or Vice-President is removed or a President shall be elected:* PROVIDED

    That whenever the powers and duties of the office of President of the United States shall devolve upon any of the persons named herein, if Congress be not then in session, or if it would not meet in accordance with law within twenty days thereafter, it shall be the duty of the person upon whom said powers and duties shall devolve to issue a proclamation convening Congress in extraordinary session, giving twenty days' notice of the time of meeting.

ELIGIBILITY.

Sec. 2. That the preceding section shall only be held to describe and apply to such officers as shall have been appointed by the advice and consent of the Senate to the offices therein named, and such as are eligible to the office of President under the Constitution, and not under impeachment by the House of Representatives of the United States at the time the powers and duties of the office shall devolve upon them respectively.

R. S. SECS. 146, 147, 148, 149, AND 150, PP. 23, 24, REPEALED.

Sec. 3. That sections one hundred and forty-six, one hundred and forty-seven, one hundred and forty-eight, one hundred and forty-nine, and one hundred and fifty of the Revised Statutes are hereby repealed.

This Act repealed the Act of 1792 and removed the President pro tempore and the Speaker of the House from the line of succession, replacing them with the Cabinet Secretaries in order of the founding of their departments, directly after the Vice President. During the 61 years the Act of 1886 was in effect, it was never activated, but there were five instances of vacancies in the Vice Presidency—Vice Presidents Theodore Roosevelt (in 1901), Calvin Coolidge (in 1923), and Harry Truman (in 1945) succeeded to the Presidency following the deaths of their predecessors; Vice Presidents Garret Hobart (in 1899) and James Sherman (in 1912) died in office—at which points the Secretary of State was next in the line of succession. In succession, they were John Hay (Secretary of State from September 1898 to July 1905), Philander C. Knox (March 1909–March 1913), Charles Evans Hughes (March 1921–March 1925), Edward Stettinius, Jr. (December 1944–June 1945), James F. Byrnes (July 1945–January 1947), and George C. Marshall (January 1947–January 1949). Joseph Grew was Acting Secretary of State from June 28 to July 3, 1945, so for that week, the next officer in line for the Presidency was actually Secretary of the Treasury Henry Morgenthau, Jr. (who was in office from January 1934 to the end of July 1945).

74. The Presidential Succession Act of 1947

Shortly after Franklin Roosevelt's death, new President Harry Truman urged Congress to update the Act of 1886, which resulted in the Presidential Succession Act of 1947 (Pub. L. 80-199, 61 Stat. 380, S. 564, enacted July 18, 1947):

AN ACT

To provide for the performance of the duties of the office of President in case of the removal, resignation, death, or inability both of the President and Vice President.

Be it enacted by the Senate and House of Representatives of the United States of America in Congress assembled, That

(a)

(1) if, by reason of death, resignation, removal from office, inability, or failure to qualify, there is neither a President nor Vice President to discharge the powers and duties of the office of President, then the Speaker of the House of Representatives shall, upon his resignation as Speaker and as Representative in Congress, act as President.

(2) The same rule shall apply in the case of the death, resignation, removal from office, or inability of an individual acting as President under this subsection.

(b) If, at the time when under subsection (a) a Speaker is to begin the discharge of the powers and duties of the office of President, there is no Speaker, or the Speaker fails to qualify as Acting President, then the President pro tempore of the Senate shall, upon his resignation as President pro tempore and as Senator, act as President.

(c) An individual acting as President under subsection (a) or subsection (b) shall continue to act until the expiration of the then current Presidential term, except that—

(1) if his discharge of the powers and duties of the office is founded in whole or in part on the failure of both the President-elect and the Vice-President-elect to qualify, then he shall act only until a President or Vice President qualifies; and

(2) if his discharge of the powers and duties of the office is founded in whole or in part on the inability of the President or Vice President, then he shall act only until the removal of the disability of one of such individuals.

(d)

(1) If, by reason of death, resignation, removal from office, inability, or failure to qualify, there is no President pro tempore to act as President under subsection (b), then the officer of the United States who is highest on the following list, and who is not under disability to discharge the powers and duties of the office of President shall act as President: Secretary of State, Secretary of the Treasury, Secretary of War, Attorney General, Postmaster General, Secretary of the Navy, Secretary of the Interior, Secretary of Agriculture, Secretary of Commerce, Secretary of Labor.

(2) An individual acting as President under this subsection shall continue so to do until the expiration of the then current Presidential term, but not after a qualified and prior-entitled individual is able to act, except that the removal of the disability of an individual higher on the list contained in paragraph (1) or the ability to qualify on the part of an individual higher on such list shall not terminate his service.

(3) The taking of the oath of office by an individual specified in the list in paragraph (1) shall be held to constitute his resignation from the office by virtue of the holding of which he qualifies to act as President.

(e) Subsections (a), (b), and (d) shall apply only to such officers as are eligible to the office of President under the Constitution.

Subsection (d) shall apply only to officers appointed, by and with the advice and consent of the Senate, prior to the time of the death, resignation, removal from office, inability, or failure to qualify, of the President pro tempore, and only to officers not under impeachment by the House of Representatives at the time the powers and duties of the office of President devolve upon them.

(f) During the period that any individual acts as President under this Act, his compensation shall be at the rate then provided by law in the case of the President.

(g) Sections 1 and 2 of the Act entitled An Act to provide for the performance of the duties of the office of President in case of the removal, death, resignation, or inability both of the President and Vice President, approved January 19, 1886 (24 Stat. 1; U. S. C., 1940 edition, title 3, secs. 21 and 22), are repealed.

This Act repealed the Act of 1886 and replaced the Congressional leaders into the line of succession, but reversed their positions from the 1792 Act, with the Speaker of the House immediately following the Vice President, and then the President pro tempore, followed by the Cabinet Secretaries in order of the founding of their departments. In 1947, the Department of Defense was created, merging the Department of War and the Department of the Navy. And then the Secretary of Defense replaced the Secretary of War in the order of succession (the Secretary of the Navy was removed from the list).

As with its predecessors, this Act has not been utilized. There have been several instances where there was no Vice President:

During the first two years this Act was in effect, President Harry Truman had no Vice President (until he was elected to his own term, and Vice President Alben Barkley was elected with him, in 1948).

There was again no Vice President following the assassination of John Kennedy in 1963, until President Lyndon Johnson was elected to his own term in 1964 with Vice President Hubert Humphrey.

75. The 25th Amendment

During Johnson's Presidency, Congress proposed the 25th Amendment, which was ratified and declared in effect in 1967. The 25th Amendment—which supersedes Article II, Section 1—reads:

Section 1. In case of the removal of the President from office or of his death or resignation, the Vice President shall become President.

Section 2. Whenever there is a vacancy in the office of the Vice President, the President shall nominate a Vice President who shall take office upon confirmation by a majority vote of both Houses of Congress.

Section 3. Whenever the President transmits to the President pro tempore of the Senate and the Speaker of the House of Representatives his written declaration that he is unable to discharge the powers and duties of his office, and until he transmits to them a written declaration to the contrary, such powers and duties shall be discharged by the Vice President as Acting President.

Section 4. Whenever the Vice President and a majority of either the principal officers of the executive departments or of such other body as Congress may by law provide, transmit to the President pro tempore of the Senate and the Speaker of the House of Representatives their written declaration that the President is unable to discharge the powers and duties of his office, the Vice President shall immediately assume the powers and duties of the office as Acting President.

Thereafter, when the President transmits to the President pro tempore of the Senate and the Speaker of the House of Representatives his written declaration that no inability exists, he shall resume the powers and duties of his office unless the Vice President and a majority of either the principal officers of the executive department or of such other body as Congress may by law provide, transmit within four days to the President pro tempore of the Senate and the

Speaker of the House of Representatives their written declaration that the President is unable to discharge the powers and duties of his office. Thereupon Congress shall decide the issue, assembling within forty-eight hours for that purpose if not in session. If the Congress, within twenty-one days after receipt of the latter written declaration, or, if Congress is not in session, within twenty-one days after Congress is required to assemble, determines by two-thirds vote of both Houses that the President is unable to discharge the powers and duties of his office, the Vice President shall continue to discharge the same as Acting President; otherwise, the President shall resume the powers and duties of his office.

This Amendment doesn't remove the need for the Presidential Succession Act, but by creating a method for filling a vacancy in the Vice Presidency midterm, it does severely limit the need for the Act.

The first two sections were invoked three times during the 1973–77 Presidential term:

1. On October 10, 1973, Vice President Spiro Agnew resigned. On October 12, President Richard Nixon nominated Representative Gerald Ford of Michigan to succeed Agnew. The Senate voted 92 to 3 to confirm Ford on November 27. On December 6, the House of Representatives confirmed Ford by a vote of 387 to 35. Ford was sworn in later that day before a joint session of the United States Congress. For the two months before Ford was sworn in, Speaker Carl Albert was next in line for the Presidency.

2. President Nixon resigned on August 9, 1974, and on that same day, Vice President Gerald Ford succeeded under the terms of the 25th Amendment (rather than Article II, as all the other succeeding Vice Presidents had).

3. Ford's succession once again created a vacancy in the Vice Presidency. On August 20, 1974, he nominated former New York Governor Nelson

Rockefeller to succeed him as Vice President. Rockefeller was confirmed by the Senate by a vote of 90 to 7 on December 10, and by the House on December 19 (287 to 128), and then sworn in that same day, in the Senate chamber. For the four months before Rockefeller was sworn in, Speaker Albert again was next in line.

Acting Presidents:

The "temporary disability" provisions of the 25th Amendment were called into use for the first time on July 12, 1985, when President Ronald Reagan underwent a colonoscopy. Because Reagan would be under anesthesia, he drafted a letter specifically invoking Section 3, granting Vice President George H.W. Bush the powers of the Acting President for a few hours. Three and a half years later, Bush would assume the full powers of the Presidency, when he was elected to succeed Reagan.

On June 29, 2002, President George W. Bush followed Reagan's precedent when he underwent his own colonoscopy, temporarily transferring his powers to Vice President Dick Cheney. He did so again on July 21, 2007.

76. Next in Line

The full list of not-the-Vice-President people who have been "next in line" for the Presidency or Presidential powers:

Under the terms of the Presidential Succession Act of 1792:

1. April 20, 1812–March 4, 1813: President pro tempore William Harris Crawford (following the death of Vice President George Clinton).

2. November 23–25, 1814: Speaker of the House Langdon Cheves (following the death of Vice President Elbridge Gerry).

3. November 25, 1814–March 4, 1817: President pro tempore John Gaillard (following his election as President pro tempore).

4. December 28, 1832–March 4, 1833: President pro tempore Hugh Lawson White (following the resignation of Vice President John C. Calhoun).

5. April 4, 1841–May 31, 1842: President pro tempore Samuel L. Southard (following the death of President William Henry Harrison).

6. May 31, 1842–March 4, 1845: President pro tempore Willie P. Mangum (following Southard's resignation and Mangum's election as President pro tempore).

7. July 9–11, 1850: There was no eligible successor available. Following the death of President Zachary Taylor, Vice President Millard Fillmore succeeded to the Presidency. There was no President pro tempore, and Speaker of the House Howell Cobb was only 34 years old (he was born in September 1815).

8. July 11, 1850–December 20, 1852: President pro tempore William R.D. King (following his election as President pro tempore); King was elected Vice President in the election of 1852.

9. December 20, 1852–March 4, 1853: President pro tempore David Rice Atchison (following King's resignation from the Senate and Atchison's election as President pro tempore).

10. April 18, 1853–December 4, 1854: President pro tempore David Rice Atchison (following the death of Vice President William R.D. King).

11. December 4–5, 1854: President pro tempore Lewis Cass (following his election as President pro tempore).

12. December 5, 1854–June 9, 1856: President pro tempore Jesse D. Bright (following his election as President pro tempore).

13. June 9–10, 1856: President pro tempore Charles E. Stuart (following his election as President pro tempore).

14. June 11, 1856–January 6, 1857: President pro tempore Jesse D. Bright (following his election as President pro tempore).

15. January 6–March 4, 1857: President pro tempore James M. Mason (following his election as President pro tempore).

16. April 15, 1865–March 2, 1867: President pro tempore Lafayette S. Foster (following the death of President Abraham Lincoln).

17. March 2, 1867–March 4, 1869: President pro tempore Benjamin F. Wade (following his election as President pro tempore).

18. November 22, 1875–March 4, 1877: President pro tempore Thomas W. Ferry (following the death of Vice President Henry Wilson).

19. September 19, 1881–October 10, 1881: There was no eligible successor available. Following the death of President James Garfield, Vice President Chester Arthur succeeded to the Presidency. The 46th Congress had adjourned in March, and the 47th was not scheduled to convene until December, so there was no President pro tempore or Speaker of the House. When Arthur arrived in Washington, he called the Senate into special session.

20. October 10–13, 1881: President pro tempore Thomas F. Bayard (following his election as President pro tempore).

21. October 13, 1881–March 4, 1885: President pro tempore David Davis III (following his election as President pro tempore).

22. November 25–December 7, 1885: There was no eligible successor available, following the death of Vice President Thomas Hendricks. The 48th Congress had adjourned in March, and the 49th did not convene until December, so there was no President pro tempore or Speaker of the House.

23. December 7, 1885–January 19, 1886: President pro tempore John Sherman (following his election as President pro tempore).

Under the terms of the Presidential Succession Act of 1886:

24. January 19, 1886–March 4, 1889: Secretary of State Thomas F. Bayard (following the adoption of the new Act, which changed the line of succession from Congressional leaders to Cabinet officers).

25. November 21, 1899–March 4, 1901: Secretary of State John Hay (following the death of Vice President Garret Hobart).

26. September 14, 1901–March 4, 1905: Secretary of State John Hay (following the death of President William McKinley).

27. October 30, 1912–March 4, 1913: Secretary of State Philander C. Knox (following the death of Vice President James Sherman).

28. August 2, 1923–March 4, 1925: Secretary of State Charles Evans Hughes (following the death of President Warren Harding).

29. April 12–June 27, 1945: Secretary of State Edward Stettinius, Jr. (following the death of President Franklin Roosevelt).

30. June 27–July 3, 1945: Secretary of the Treasury Henry Morgenthau, Jr. (following the resignation of Secretary of State Edward Stettinius, Jr.).

31. July 3, 1945–January 21, 1947: Secretary of State James F. Byrnes (following his appointment as Secretary of State).

32. January 21–July 17, 1947: Secretary of State George C. Marshall (following Byrnes's resignation and Marshall's appointment as Secretary of State).

Under the terms of the Presidential Succession Act of 1947:

33. July 17, 1947–January 3, 1949: Speaker of the House Joseph William Martin, Jr. (following the adoption of the new Act, which changed the line of succession from Cabinet officers to Congressional leaders).

34. January 3–January 20, 1949: Speaker of the House Sam Rayburn (following his election as Speaker of the House).

35. November 22, 1963–January 20, 1965: Speaker of the House John William McCormack (following the death of President John Kennedy).

36. October 10–December 6, 1973: Speaker of the House Carl Albert (following the resignation of Vice President Spiro Agnew).

37. August 9–December 19, 1974: Speaker of the House Carl Albert (following the resignation of President Richard Nixon).

Invocations of the 25th Amendment:

38. July 13, 1985: Speaker of the House Thomas P. O'Neill, Jr. (when President Ronald Reagan transferred powers to Acting President George H.W. Bush).

39. June 29, 2002: Speaker of the House Dennis Hastert (when President George W. Bush transferred powers to Acting President Dick Cheney).

40. July 21, 2007: Speaker of the House Nancy Pelosi (when President George W. Bush transferred powers to Acting President Dick Cheney).

77. Designated Survivor

Four of the nine Presidential vacancies have been the result of assassination, but in the modern era, more thought has been spent on the possibility that the President and other people in the line of succession would die simultaneously, leaving multiple vacancies. And though we might assume such thinking dates only to 2001 and the beginning of the War on Terror, in fact, those who think the unthinkable in order to prepare for it have been doing so since at least the Cold War. The Senate Historical Office says, "the practice of one Cabinet official remaining absent from [the State of the Union address] dates at least to the early 1960s and perhaps much earlier. Prior to the 1980s, however, the selection of the official was often not made public." In the modern era, the practice of designating a survivor or successor has been extended to other group events, including Inauguration Day, in order to keep at least one member of the legal line of succession safe. Only Cabinet members who are eligible to succeed to the Presidency are chosen as designated survivors. The designated survivor is provided Presidential-level security and transport for the duration of the event, and an aide accompanies the designated survivor with the nuclear football.

Perhaps the youngest designated survivor was Secretary of Agriculture Mike Espy, who stayed away from the 1994 State of the Union address by President Bill Clinton. At the time, Espy was 40 years, 56 days old. He served as the 25th Secretary of Agriculture from January 1993 to December 1994, after representing Mississippi in the House of Representatives for six years.

Slightly older than Espy was Secretary of Housing and Urban Development Andrew Cuomo, who was 41 years, 44 days old on January 19, 1999, for another State of the Union address. He was in the Cabinet from January 1997 to January 2001, and would later serve as the 56th Governor of New York, beginning in 2011. Had the unthinkable happened on those days, either would have been younger than the youngest President in history, Theodore Roosevelt (who took office two months before his 43rd birthday).

The Senate's list of designated survivors for State of the Union and other joint addresses to Congress dates back to 1984 and includes six each Secretaries of Agriculture and the Interior; four Secretaries of Energy and of Commerce (well, three, but Donald Evans was named twice, in 2004 and 2005); three each Secretaries of HUD and Attorneys General; two Secretaries of Transportation; and one Secretary of Health and Human Services (Donna Shalala, who was the first woman to be named designated survivor, in January 1996). Additionally, since 2005, there have been designated survivors named for Presidential Inaugurations: Secretary of the Interior Gale Norton, Secretary of Defense Robert Gates (who was bridging Republican and Democratic Administrations, staying on from George W. Bush's term to Barack Obama's), and Secretary of Veterans Affairs Eric Shinseki.

SUMMATIONS

78. The Most Common Vice Presidents (Those Appearing in the Fewest Lists in This Book)

Considering ranked lists, three are tied with no appearances whatsoever:

ADLAI E. STEVENSON (1893–97)
CALVIN COOLIDGE (1921–23)
SPIRO T. AGNEW (1969–73)

Eleven more Vice Presidents appear on one list each:

THOMAS JEFFERSON (1797–1801): The Five Vice Presidents Who Outlived Their Wives by the Longest Time (he's ranked #2).

RICHARD M. JOHNSON (1837–41): The Vice Presidents Who Were Older Than the Greatest Number of Their Predecessors (tied for #4).

GEORGE M. DALLAS (1845–49): The Five Vice Presidents Who Had the Most Children (tied for #4).

SCHUYLER COLFAX (1869–73): The Five Vice Presidents Who Had the Fewest Children (tied for #4).

CHESTER ARTHUR (1881): The Five Vice Presidents Who Died the Youngest (#5).

CHARLES W. FAIRBANKS (1905–09): The Five Presidents Who Were the Most Younger Than Their Wives (#6).

JAMES S. SHERMAN (1909–12): The Five Vice Presidents Who Died the Youngest (#4).

LYNDON B. JOHNSON (1961–63): The Five Vice Presidents Who Predeceased Their Wives by the Longest Time (#2).

HUBERT H. HUMPHREY (1965–69): The Five Vice Presidents Who Outlived Their Wives by the Longest Time (tied for #2).

GEORGE H.W. BUSH (1981–89): The Five Vice Presidents Who Lived the Longest (#4).

DICK CHENEY (2001–09): The Vice Presidents Who Were Older Than the Greatest Number of Their Predecessors (tied for #4).

79. The Most Uncommon Vice Presidents (Those Appearing in the Most Lists in This Book)

Considering only ranked lists, there are three Vice Presidents making appearances on six different lists, so ranking them based on their appearances on those lists yields:

1. WILLIAM RUFUS DEVANE KING (1853): The Vice Presidents Who Were Older Than the Greatest Number of Their Predecessors (he's tied for #2 on that list); The Vice Presidents Who Had the Fewest Children (tied for #1); The Oldest Vice Presidents (#4); The Vice Presidents Who Were the Greatest Number of Years Older Than Their Predecessors (#2); The Vice Presidents Who Were the Greatest Number of Years Older Than Their Presidents (#2); and The Vice Presidents Who Served the Shortest Terms (#3).

2. HANNIBAL HAMLIN (1861–65): The Vice Presidents Who Outlived the Greatest Number of Their Successors (#1); The Vice Presidents Who Had the Greatest Number of Living Predecessors (tied for #2); Ten Vice Presidents Who Were the Most Older Than Their Wives (#3 among those with second wives); The Five Vice Presidents Who Predeceased Their Wives by the Longest Time (#2 among those with second wives); The Five Vice Presidents Who Outlived Their Wives by the Longest Time (#5); and The Five Vice Presidents Who Were the Greatest Number of Years Older Than Their Predecessors (#3).

3. AARON BURR (1801–05): The Five Vice Presidents Who Lived the Longest after Leaving Office (#4); The Vice Presidents Who Outlived the Greatest Number of Their Successors (tied for #3); Ten Vice Presidents

Who Were the Most Older Than Their Wives (#5 among those with second wives); The Five Presidents Who Were the Most Younger Than Their Wives (#1, in regard to his first wife); The Five Vice Presidents Who Predeceased Their Wives by the Longest Time (#4 among those with second wives); and The Five Vice Presidents Who Outlived Their Wives by the Longest Time (#4 in regard to his first wife).

Six Vice Presidents appear on five ranked lists each, but ranking them based on their positions on the lists yields:

4. NELSON ROCKEFELLER (1974–77): The Five Vice Presidents Who Died the Soonest after Leaving Office (#2); The Vice Presidents Who Were Older Than the Greatest Number of Their Predecessors (#1); The Five Presidents Who Were the Most Younger Than Their Wives (#3); The Five Vice Presidents Who Predeceased Their Wives by the Longest Time (#1 among those with second wives); and The Five Oldest Vice Presidents (#5).

5. RICHARD M. NIXON (1953–61): The Vice Presidents Who Lived the Longest after Leaving Office (#2), The Vice Presidents Who Outlived the Greatest Number of Their Successors (tied for #3); The Five Presidents Who Were the Most Younger Than Their Wives (#4); The Youngest Vice Presidents (#2); and The Vice Presidents Who Were the Greatest Number of Years Younger Than Their Predecessors (#1); Nixon is among the most common Presidents, appearing on only two lists in that book.

6. LEVI P. MORTON (1889–93): The Five Vice Presidents Who Lived the Longest (#2); The Vice Presidents Who Outlived the Greatest Number of Their Successors (#2); Ten Vice Presidents Who Were the Most Older Than Their Wives (he appears twice on this list, at #4 for both his first wife and his second wife); and The Five Vice Presidents Who Outlived Their Wives by the Longest Time (#1).

7. DANIEL D. TOMPKINS (1817–25): The Five Vice Presidents Who Died the Youngest (#1); The Five Vice Presidents Who Died the Soonest after Leaving Office (#1); The Five Vice Presidents Who Had the Most Children (tied for #4); The Five Youngest Vice Presidents (#5); and The Five Vice Presidents Who Were the Greatest Number of Years Younger Than Their Predecessors (#3).

8. THOMAS R. MARSHALL (1913–21): The Five Vice Presidents Who Died the Soonest After Leaving Office (#5); The Vice Presidents Who Were Older Than the Greatest Number of Their Predecessors (tied for #4); The Five Vice Presidents Who Had the Fewest Children (tied for #1); Ten Vice Presidents Who Were the Most Older Than Their Wives (#1); and The Five Vice Presidents Who Predeceased Their Wives by the Longest Time (#4).

9. HENRY WILSON (1873–75): The Vice Presidents Who Were Older Than the Greatest Number of Their Predecessors (tied for #4); The Vice Presidents Who Had the Greatest Number of Living Predecessors (tied for #2); The Five Vice Presidents Who Had the Fewest Children (tied for #4); Ten Vice Presidents Who Were the Most Older Than Their Wives (#3); and The Five Vice Presidents Who Were the Greatest Number of Years Older Than Their Predecessors (#4).

INDEX

of people appearing in this book (by chapter/list number, not by page). Bold-faced numbers indicate lists in which the person appears. Numbers not in bold face are supporting characters.

Blaine, James G.: 36, 55, **67**, 68

Blair, Francis: 55

Blount, Winton: 70

Blumenthal, W. Michael: 64

Bonaparte, Charles J.: 70, 71

Booth, John Wilkes: 47, 72

Bowen, Otis R.: 58

Boyd, Alan Stephenson: **60**

Bradford, William: **59**, 61

Brady, John R.: 36

Breckinridge, John (grandfather of the Vice President): 59, 61

Breckinridge, John C. (Vice President): **2**, **5**, **6**, 7, 8, 15, 17, 18, 20, 21, **26**, 31, 33, 34, **40**, 42, **43**, 48, 52, 53, 61

Breckinridge, Mary Cyrene Burch (Second Lady): 26

Bright, Jesse D.: 76

Brown, Aaron V.: 61

Brown, Ron: 61

Bryan, William Jennings: 55

Buchanan, James (President): 2, 5, 35, 36, 40, 41, 44, 48, 53, 56, 66, 67, 69, **70**

Burr, Aaron (Vice President): The Vice Presidents, **3**, **5**, 6, 10, **14**, **24**, **25**, **26**, **27**, 28, 31, 33, 35, 41, 42, 45, 50, 52, 53, 57, 79

Burr, Eliza Bowen Jumel (Second Lady): 24, 26, 28

Burr, Theodosia Bartow Prevost (Second Lady): 25, 27, 28

Bush, George H.W. (Vice President & President): **1**, 3, **5**, **6**, 7, 17, 18, 31, 33, 35, 36, 40, 43, 46, 49, 52, 55, 56, 75, 76, 78

Bush, George W. (President): 5, 38, 52, 53, 68, **70**, 75, 76, 77

Butz, Earl L.: **58**

Byrd, Harry F.: 35

Byrnes, James F.: 73, 76

Calhoun, Floride Bonneau Colhoun (Second Lady): 22, 24

Calhoun, John C. (Vice President): 5, **6**, 17, 18, 19, 20, **22**, **24**, 31, 33, 34, 35, 40, 41, 46, 48, 49, 50, **51**, 52, 55, 65, **67**, 69, 72, 76

Cameron, James Donald: 60, 71

Cameron, Simon: 71

Campbell, George Washington: 64

Carter, James Earl "Jimmy" (President): 3, 35, 36, 53, 55, 56, 67

Cass, Lewis: 35, 36, 53, **56**, 76

Celebrezze, Anthony J.: 64

Chao, Elaine: 64, 70

Cheney, Richard Bruce "Dick" (Vice President): 3, **5**, **6**, **15**, 17, 18, 31, 33, 41, 46, 49, 55, 75, 76, 78

Cheves, Langdon: 76

Claiborne, William Charles Cole: 54

Clark, Ramsey: 60

Clary, Joseph: 32

Clay, Henry: 36, 50, 55

Cleveland, Grover (President): 15, **21**, 36, 41, 44, 45, 47, 48, 52, 55, 66, 68

Clifford, Clark: 29

Clifford, Nathan: 68

Clinton, George (Vice President): 3, 5, **6**, 7, 8, 9, 10, 13, 14, **15**, 24, 32, 33, 35, 39, 40, **42**, 44, 45, 48, 49, 50, 51, 52, 53, 65, 72, 76

Clinton, William Jefferson "Bill" (President): 3, 5, 13, 34, 35, 53, 56, **70**, 77

Cobb, Howell: 76

Coleman, Norman Jay: **66**

Coleman, William Thaddeus Jr.: **58**

Colfax, Ella M. Wade (Second Lady): 28, 29

Colfax, Evelyn Clark (Second Lady): 23, 28, 29

Colfax, Schuyler P. (Vice President): 7, 8, 12, 13, 14, 15, 17, 18, 20, **23**, 28,